The
Talbot
Press
books

FROM THE LAND OF DREAMS

CONTENTS

JOHN TODHUNTER.

The author of this volume of Irish poems, most of which are now published for the first time, died, after a long period of failing health, at his home in Bedford Park, London, on October 25th, 1916.

In that home he had lived and worked for thirty-four years, during which a young generation grew up in Ireland—a generation that knew little or nothing of his personality, though it was by no means indifferent to such Irish offshoots of his poetic work as found their way across the Channel. This volume will show how deeply he was interested in Irish themes, and how much of thought and passion he put into his treatment of them. All his lyrical pieces on Ireland are here, as well as a fine narrative poem on the tragic theme of the Death of Conlaoch. It is a legacy to Ireland which his countrymen will surely value as it deserves, and which it may be hoped will awaken interest in the whole of his literary career as well as in a character of rare attractiveness.

I wish it were possible by any literary art to take the readers of this memoir into the atmosphere which one breathed in the companionship of John Todhunter. Few men so gentle and unassertive have ever, I think, so decidedly made the atmosphere, set the keynote of the company in which they happened to be ; particularly, of course, if this were in his own home. The spirit of beauty hovered about him and his belongings ;

the grace of things old and simple but fine and delicate, the dignity of thought and scholarship, and above all the noble attraction of a sincere and free spirit. One saw him at his best, perhaps, at the Friday evening " Symposia " which went on at his house during the winter months. Friends old and new used to gather there, most of them men who had made a mark in some sphere of life ; but whether they were brilliant men or everyday men, eminent or unknown, unlearned or full of out-of-the-way lore, Todhunter's quiet geniality, his true Irish hospitality, courtesy and kindness, made them all feel at home and brought out whatever was best in their nature or their talent. A kettle at these times sang cheerfully on the hob, and punch was made with a certain ritual and with old-fashioned utensils such as used to adorn the tables of our grandfathers when the cloth was cleared away and when the old silver, the pile of lemons, the decanters and long-stemmed glasses, were sombrely reflected in the shining mahogany which was an Irish gentleman's pride. At Todhunter's house there were also long clay pipes, a reminiscence of the earlier symposia of the Rhymers' Club at the " Cheshire Cheese ;" and we talked of all things in heaven and earth, but most often, I think, of poetry or history, till the inexorable distances of London made us separate to catch our trains at Turnham Green.

What most impressed me, I think, about Todhunter's personality was that I have seldom known anyone whose whole life, both the spiritual and the outward life, was cast so much in one mould. The distinction of his life was its harmony. He was a man who had the rare gift of style—it was in everything he wrote, in the surroundings he made for himself, in his talk and

in his very look. And this style was really the man.
About him there was never the least trace of pose or
strain. He loved his art—the art of a fine craftsman
in literature—and reverenced it far too much to use it
for the expression of anything he did not thoroughly
care for and believe in. He might have been more
popular if he had been less sincere; but he chose the
path which among those who knew him will always
crown his memory with a peculiar honour. Among
contemporary writers there was one other who gave
something of the same impression of personal dignity,
loyalty, and harmony—also a fellow-countryman, and
one whose friendship I was privileged to possess. I
speak of Aubrey de Vere.

Todhunter's outward life was uneventful. He came
of a Quaker stock, originally from Cumberland. They
were seafaring folk. His great-grandfather was a
Whitehaven shipowner who sailed his own ships. On
one occasion he was presented by the underwriters of
Liverpool with a piece of plate in recognition of his
seamanship and gallantry in saving the ship *Ellen* in
difficult circumstances.

John Todhunter's grandfather settled in Dublin in
the timber trade, and had a house on Sir John Roger-
son's Quay, where, on December 30, 1839, the poet
was born. His mother was one of the Limerick
Harveys, and through these relations he made
acquaintance as a boy with West of Ireland scenery.
His maternal uncle, Reuben, had a house on the
Shannon, with some fine pictures and a beautiful old
garden. He went to school first at Mountmellick, and
afterwards at the Friends' School, York. When the
serious business of life began for him—it began at
sixteen years of age—we find him working in

business houses in Dublin, Pim's and Bewley's; but before long he gravitated to Trinity College, where he entered the Medical School. Hard work in this field obliged him to give up what he called "my dream of Honors in English Literature," but he contrived to win three times in succession the important Vice-Chancellor's Prize for English Verse, as well as the Gold Medal of the University Philosophical Society. In 1866 his poem "In a Gondola" was accepted by Thackeray for the *Cornhill*. He read at this time widely and eagerly, and among the English poets one can see that Keats had a deep influence on his poetic diction, though when he came later under the spell of the severer muse of Shelley he declared that he exuded enormous quantities of liquid Keats in the process of forming his style on a more athletic model. He had evidently also been much impressed by the thought and style of William Blake. Certain poems in his first volume, "Laurella," are not only full of the mystical feeling, but intentionally echo the manner of Blake. He now began to form literary friendships. Edward Dowden, Standish O'Grady, Alfred Perceval Graves, Edmund and George Armstrong, C. E. Fitzgerald, the famous oculist, and J. B. Yeats, father of the poet, were among his contemporaries and intimates. Unhappily at this time the shadow of ill-health began to fall across his life, partly from overwork, partly constitutional delicacy. He was never at any time robust, and though he showed it as little as possible, he was often seriously ailing in his later years, a fact which accounts for the comparative retirement in which he lived after settling in London.

His profession of medicine, though it was not his "dream," and though the dream, in the end, asserted its complete dominion over his life, was practised both earnestly and successfully. The author of a short obituary notice, whom I hope it may be allowed to identify as Sir J. W. Moore, writes of him as follows :

"When the author of this brief memoir entered the wards of the Meath Hospital and County Dublin Infirmary as a medical student in the winter session of 1866, he found John Todhunter acting as Clinical Clerk to two great physicians, William Stokes and Alfred Hudson—men who were the complement of each other : Stokes, the philosophic physician ; Hudson, the keen observer and the skilled and resourceful therapeutist.

"Todhunter took the neophyte by the hand, initiated him into the mysteries of bedside teaching and learning, taught him the rudiments of clinical medicine, by his conduct and example brought home to his mind the solemnity of the work in which teacher and taught were engaged, and showed him in a practical way how precious a privilege it is to minister to the sick and suffering. Small wonder, therefore, that the writer remembers those far-off days with gratitude and pleasure."

He took his M.B. degree in 1867 and the M.D. in 1871, studied medicine for some time in Vienna and Paris (with many side-glances to music and painting), and was appointed Visiting Physician to Cork Street Fever Hospital. In May, 1870, he had married Miss Ball—a sister of the late Sir Robert Ball, the well-known astronomer—but had to mourn her death a few months later. His second marriage, to Miss Dora L. Digby, took place in 1879.

But the year 1870, besides his marriage, was marked by the first step towards the calling to which he afterwards devoted himself exclusively. In that year he became Professor of English Literature at Alexandra College, Dublin. In 1892 he produced, in the course of his work in this capacity, a remarkable critical essay called "A Theory of the Beautiful," which is treated with much respect by the German philosopher, Schasler, in his "Kritische Geschichte der Æsthetik." In this study Todhunter develops the theory that harmony, or the attempt to reach it, is the chief common feature in all the protean forms of beauty. This harmony is of such a nature as to form a kind of trichord—it produces in us a triple sensation compounded of melancholy, of joy and of worship. These three elements are all accounted for by the conception of beauty as the eternal quest for an unattainable ideal. Art endeavours to frame a kosmos out of chaos, to reveal by means of imperfect symbols the divine perfection. The melancholy which is ever associated with the highest and noblest art is the sense of this imperfection; the joy resides in the ardour of the half-victorious struggle to overcome and harmonise it; the worship is paid to the transitory but unforgettable gleams of truth and light which now and then touch with an unearthly glory the highest achievements of the painter, the poet or the musician.

In this admirable essay, strictly meditated and finely expressed, Todhunter may be said to have found his feet. He knew now where his real path lay, and giving up the regular practice of his profession he devoted himself to literature.

A period of travel, which took him to Italy and even as far as Egypt, now followed. During this time he gave much thought and zeal to the study of painting, and now and all his life, since as a boy he first heard a performance of the "Messiah" in St. Patrick's Cathedral, he was an intense lover and student of

music. The volume of poems on music, called
"Sounds and Sweet Airs," contains some of his
most precise and imaginative work.* It was a
productive period in literature. He lectured on
Italian art. His first volume of poems, "Laurella,"
appeared in 1876. It was marked by grace, ten-
derness and melody, but so far I think his critical
prose work remained the more mature—on that side
he ripened earlier than in poetry. His first play, a
thoughtful and graceful study on the classical theme
of the death and recovery of Alcestis, appeared in
1879, and in the following year came a prose book,
"A Study of Shelley," which showed not only sensitive
appreciation but a very keen and sane judgment. He
left Dublin for London in 1874, and in 1881 settled
finally in the house he had built for himself in Bedford
Park. But if he thus quitted Ireland in person, he
soon came nearer to it in spirit. His early life and his
education in Trinity College had done little or nothing
to bring him into touch with Irish literature or tradition. "Laurella" showed no trace of these influences.
They first appeared in the volume entitled "The Banshee," published in 1888. The dedication to Standish
O'Grady, "whose epic history of Ireland first gave me
an interest in our bardic tales," shows to whom Todhunter, like many another of his contemporaries, owed
the revelation of the beauty and power of the mythical
literature of Ireland. It is one of my own early recol-
lections of our friendship to have heard Todhunter, a
year or so before the publication of this volume, read the
"Sons of Turenn" to O'Grady and myself in a lonely
house among the Wicklow hills, within sound of the
"warbling Annamoe," celebrated later by O'Grady

---

* These poems were not published in collected form till 1905.

B

himself in his great story of " Red Hugh's Captivity." The " Banshee " volume contained, besides the " Lamentation for the Sons of Turenn," a poetic version of the " Tale of the Children of Lir," and a striking lyric, perhaps in Ireland the best known of his pieces, the dirge called " Aghadoe." In 1896 came the volume entitled " Three Irish Bardic Tales," in which the famous trilogy was completed by adding to the " Lamentation " and the " Children of Lir " the story of Deirdre and the Sons of Usnach. That his interest in Ireland was not confined to the region of myth and poetry is shown by the excellent and carefully studied " Life of Sarsfield," which he contributed to the New Irish Library in 1894. Finally—to complete this brief account of his Irish work—we have the present volume, " From the Land of Dreams." Here we have examples, old and new, of his lyrical genius at its very best. I may mention particularly the rich music of the verses entitled " Irish Melodies," inscribed to the memory of the celebrated singer, Catherine Hayes; the beautiful series of meditative poems called " Dreams in Exile," and the very fine and moving narrative of the " Death of Connlaoch," the Celtic version of a theme which appears in the primitive literature of several Aryan peoples—the death of a gallant son at the unwitting hands of his father.

To return to the work done under other than Irish inspiration, I may mention the two classical plays, " Helena in Troas " (1886) and " A Sicilian Idyll " (1891), both of which were performed in public; and a verse drama called " The Poison-Flower," written on a weird and ghastly theme of the Italian Renaissance. " Helena " was something of an event in the literary and theatrical world. To see Poetry brought back to the stage in his day, and partly perhaps by his means, had long been a hope of Todhunter's; and the performance of this drama on a beautiful Greek stage constructed by Godwin, with Hermann Vezin, Mr. and Mrs. Tree, and Miss Alma Murray filling the principal parts, was an experiment in this direction. It was hardly a successful one. There was much more of poetry than of stage in the play, and the strict Greek form in which it was cast, though interesting to the scholar, must have been a handicap with a modern audience. The performance attracted considerable attention both at home and in France and Germany, but the "Sicilian Idyll," though a slighter piece of work, seems to me more charming and effectual as a realisation of "poetry on the stage." I had the pleasure of seeing it on its first private performance at Bedford Park. It was afterwards put on at the Vaudeville, as was also the "Poison-Flower," but owing partly to mistakes of management neither of them made the mark it should have done on its intrinsic merits.

In 1893 he broke entirely new ground with a prose drama, "The Black Cat," which was produced by the Independent Theatre. This was evidently written under the influence of Ibsen, and was in fact one of the first plays, if not the very first, to show evidence of that influence on the English stage. There are four principal characters : the painter, Denham; his wife; their little daughter, Undine, and Blanche Tremaine, an old school friend of Mrs. Denham's, who, after making, as she says, rather a mess of her life, comes into the Denham household to make a much greater mess of that. She is portrayed as a type of the witch-woman, enthralling and poisonous, and is presented without much subtlety or originality.

It is to the portrayal of the wife that the author has given his full powers, and the result is a very remarkable and penetrating study of character. Mrs. Denham is one of those persons who reverse the attribute of Mephistopheles; she is always longing to do the right thing and always does the wrong. She is a self-torturing woman, with a heart full of love which some crust that has formed over her nature will never let her express: to her daughter she seems a persecutor; to her husband, a troublesome and thwarting enigma. She tries to live by principles, trampling down her human instincts, and at last reaches such a state of alienation from all her little world that she can no longer endure the solitude she has created around her; she takes poison and dies. The play, as I have said, is distinctly an Ibsenite piece—Ibsenite in its irony, its symbolism, in the bitter quality of its tragic end, and in the way in which the tragedy is gradually developed through acts and conversations of the most everyday character; but it is no mere reflection of another's genius—it is the method of Ibsen applied to a theme conceived with freshness and originality; and although there are weak places in its construction, it has life enough to be interesting even now when the Scandinavian drama has ceased to exert any spell save that which may be due to the bygone eccentricities of the British theatrical censorship. But the most successful of his plays on the stage was one which he wrote in collaboration with Edward Rose, " Mary Queen of Scots." This was frequently played in the provinces and also at the Globe Theatre by T. Thalberg's company, the part of the Queen being taken by Marion Terry.

Some of Todhunter's least known but most attractive

work was done in connection with that distinguished
Literary Society, the "Sette of Odde Volumes," which
he joined, I think, in the early nineties. It used to
meet at Limmer's famous restaurant, immortalised in
Thackeray's lines :—

"My name is John Collins, head-waiter at Limmer's
    At the corner of Conduck Street, Hanover Square,
And my chief occupation is filling up brimmers
    For thirsty young gentlemen burdened with care.'

Members used to be called on by the President, "His
Oddship," to read essays, which were afterwards dis-
cussed with a great deal of chaff and good-humoured
satire, and several of Todhunter's have been printed in
small volumes, one of which contains a capital drawing
by Hassall of the author in search of a subject. These
little essays are full of poetic feeling, of knowledge
gleaned in unfrequented by-ways, and of fine literary
criticism, and they contain some of the most admirable
prose written in our day. I cannot forbear quoting one
short passage on the style of Francis Bacon :—

"Bacon was a wise man, and he embodies his
wisdom in gnomic sentences, which have the hard
outline of graven gems. His wisdom is that of a man
of wide outward experience, and finely cultivated
common sense. The material world was to him
opake and solid. He did not feel, as Blake did, that
it was but a veil, wherein we see and touch the
pulsating wings of a ' covering cherub.' His periods
march like a Roman army, with captains mailed in
gold, and centurions clothed in scarlet, to the sound
of brazen trumpets, as they go forth to order the
provinces of Knowledge under the standards of
Reason."*

Todhunter's last important work was a translation of

---

* From "An Essay upon Essays," 1890.

Heine's " Buch der Lieder " (1907), in which he has gone nearer, I think, than any other English poet to catching the inimitable grace of that wonderful lyrist. His rendering of the " Pilgrimage to Kevlaar " is a veritable gem of verse-translation.*

I do not pretend to give here a complete bibliography of Todhunter's works. For that, so far as they appeared in book form, the reader may consult that invaluable publication which it is to be hoped every Irish man of letters has at hand, *The Irish Book Lover*, in its issue for December and January, 1916-1917. But it will be seen that he laboured faithfully in his calling, and left behind him a considerable body of literary achievement. It gives, as a whole, a deep impression of sincerity, dignity and delicacy, and behind it all one divines a keen and manly intellect. It is good to live awhile in the companionship of such work. I hope we may some day see a collected edition of the best things in his prose and verse. It would be a welcome addition to the literary treasures of modern Ireland.

Todhunter's was a well-filled life, a life of much toil carried on with quiet but unflagging persistence in the face of constant illness; but a life, also, of much happiness in his work, in his friends, and, above all, in his home. In spite of his long residence in London, he never forgot his country; and perhaps no praise could please him better—certainly none could be more true— than to say that he gave Ireland cause to remember him with affection and pride.

T. W. ROLLESTON.

---

* As published it is marred by an unlucky misprint. In the stanza about the Virgin, who

> . . . bending over the sick man,
> Lightly her heart did lay
> Upon his heart, and gently
> She smiled and vanished away,

the first " heart " should be " hand."

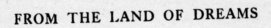

FROM THE LAND OF DREAMS

DEDICATION

I

For all my fellow-countrymen,
    And women, East or West,
For every kindly Irish heart
    Within an Irish breast ;

II

All exiles for the Old Land who long,
    And those whose destinies
Have held them in that Land of Dreams,
    Knowing no other skies ;

III

For all abroad, and all at home,
    My songs to every wind
I breathe, in hope one song of mine
    One Irish heart may find.

FROM THE LAND OF DREAMS

THE BANSHEE

I

Green in the wizard arms of the foam-bearded
    Atlantic,
An Isle of old enchantment, a melancholy Isle,
Enchanted and dreaming lies ;
And there, by Shannon's flowing,
In the moonlight, spectre-thin,
The spectre Erin sits.

II

An aged Desolation
She broods by old Shannon's flowing,
A mother of many children, of children exiled
    and dead ;
In her home, with bent head, homeless,
Clasping her knees she sits,
Keening, keening !

III

And at her keene the fairy-grass
Trembles on dun and barrow ;
Around the foot of her ancient crosses
The grave-grass shakes and the nettle swings ;
In haunted glens the meadow-sweet

Flings to the nightwind
Her mystic, mournful perfume ·
The sad spearmint by holy wells
Breathes melancholy balm.

IV

Sometimes she lifts her head,
With blue eyes, tearless,
And gazes athwart the reek of night
Upon things long past,
Upon things to come.

V

And sometimes when the moon
Brings tempest upon the deep,
And roused Atlantic thunders from his caverns
        in the West,
The wolf-hound at her feet
Springs up with a mighty bay,
And chords of mystery sound from the wild
        harp at her side,
Strung from the hearts of poets ;
And she flies on the wings of tempest
Around her shuddering Isle,
    With grey hair streaming :
A meteor of evil omen,
The spectre of hope forlorn,
Keening, keening !

VI

She keenes, and the strings of her wild harp
    shiver
On the gusts of night :
O'er the Four Waters she keenes—over Moyle
    she keenes,
O'er the Sea of Milith, and the Strait of Strong-
    bow,
And the Ocean of Columbus.

VII

And the Fianna hear, and the ghosts of her cloudy
    hovering heroes ;
And the Swan Fianola wails o'er the waters of
    Innisfail,
Chanting her song of destiny, the rune of the
    weaving Fates.

VIII

And the nations hear, in the void and quaking-
    time of night,
Sad unto dawning, dirges,
And snatches of bardic song ;
Their souls quake in the void and quaking-time
    of night,
And they dream of the weird of kings,
Of tyrannies moulting, sick
In the dreadful wind of change.

IX

Wail no more, lonely one, Mother of Exiles, wail
    no more,

Banshee of the World—no more !

Thy sorrows are the world's, thou art no more
    alone,

Thy wrongs the world's !

LYRICS AND BALLADS

AN INVOCATION

O Memory, Nurse of Dreams, out of the night
Steal to my hearth, and by the autumn fire
Crouch like a Fairy woman, and fan the turf,
Fan the sweet Irish sods until they glow !
Then lay thine ear close to thy sounding
    shell,
And listen, till within its winding caves
The words of mystery wake ; and to my spirit,
Roaming the shadowy halls of lonely thought,
Where deep it dwells, lamped by a sibylline
    star,
Come visions of the never dying past.

A golden youth flames in thy hoary hair
And withered cheek, and all the world grows
    young
In the soft shining of thy dream-lit eyes.
Thou art the grave Recording Angel, calm
As a bright cloud of dawn, and in thy voice
The eternal deep that lies behind me calls
To the eternal deep that lies before.

IRISH MUSIC

(Inscribed to the memory of Catherine Hayes)

I

A voice beside the dim enchanted river,
  Out of the twilight, where the brooding trees
Hear Shannon's druid waters chant for ever
  Tales of dead Kings, and Bards, and Shana-
    chies ;
A girl's young voice out of the twilight, singing
  Old songs beside a legendary stream,
A girl's clear voice, o'er the wan waters ringing,
  Beats with its wild wings at the Gates of Dream.

II

The flagger-leaves whereon shy dewdrops glisten
  Are swaying, swaying gently to the sound,
The meadow-sweet and spearmint, as they listen,
  Breathe wistfully their wizard balm around ;
And there, alone with her lone heart and heaven,
  Thrushlike she sings and lets her voice go free,
Her soul, of all its hidden longing shriven,
  Soars on wild wings with her wild melody.

III

Sweet in its plaintive Irish modulations,
  Her fresh young voice tuned to old sorrow
    seems,

The passionate cry of countless generations
 Keenes in her breast as there she sings and
  dreams.
No more, sad voice ; for now the dawn is break-
  ing,
 Through the long night, through Ireland's
  night of tears,
New songs wake in the morn of her awaking
 From the enchantment of nine hundred years.

SONGS TO OLD IRISH AIRS

THE LAMENT OF AIDEEN FOR OSCUR

(Air : " The Gaol of Clonmel.")

I

The wan woods are quailing
  In the wind of their sorrow,
  Their keene they might borrow
From the voice of my wailing.
  My bed's the cold stone
By the dark flowing river
  Ochone-a-rie ! Ochone !
Thou art gone, and for ever.

II

Ah ! why didst thou love me
  But to leave me despairing,
  My anguish outstaring
The bleak heaven above me ?
  I lie all alone
Where hope's morning comes never
  Ochone-a-rie ! Ochone !
I have lost thee for ever.

III

The dumb grave mocks my raving,
 From the dead comes no token
 Where thy good sword lies broken
Thou art cold to my craving !
 We may lie down and moan,
But our champion wakes never.
 Ochone-a-rie !   Ochone !
We are fallen for ever.

EILEEN'S FAREWELL

(To an old Irish Air)

I

 Ring out my knell,
Ye walls and towers of Neil Dhuv !
 Farewell, O farewell
Evermore to the fields that I love !
 For the world, the world is dreary—
Let me lie with my baby alone,
 The heart that is weary
Rests only under the stone.

II

 Think on my doom,
And weep for pity, Neil Dhuv !
 On the slab of my tomb
No name be graven but Love !

c

With the winds, in places lonely,
My name of sorrow shall dwell,
And I sigh to them only
To waft thee Eileen's farewell.

DREAMS IN EXILE

I

LONGING

I

Oh ! the sunshine of old Ireland when it lies
  On her woods and on her waters,
And gleams through her soft skies
  Tenderly as the lovelight in her daughters'
      Faithful eyes !

II

Oh ! the brown streams of old Ireland, how they
    leap
  From her glens, and fill their hollows
With wild song, till charmed to sleep
  By the murmuring bees in meadows where the
    swallows
      Glance and sweep !

III

Oh ! my home there in old Ireland, the old ways
  We had when I knew only
The ways of one sweet place ;
  Ere, afar from all I loved, I wandered lonely
      Many days.

IV

Oh ! the springtime in old Ireland ! O'er the sea
  I can smell our hawthorn bushes,
And it all comes back to me—
    The sweet air, the old place, the trees, the
      cows, the thrushes
        Mad with glee.

V

I'm weary for old Ireland ! Once again
  To see her fields before me
In sunshine or in rain ;
    And the longing in my heart, as it comes o'er
      me,
        Stings like pain.

II

SPRING

I

Oh ! the flowers, the Irish flowers of my visionary
    home,
  In the fields where I wandered, where I wan-
      dered as a boy !
In the meads where they were growing I could
    see the Shannon flowing,
  And growing still I see them, and my heart
    grows young in joy,

In the sunny fields of memory ever in splendour
    blowing,
  Where Time's grey wings no shadow cast, the
    young hours to annoy.

II

Oh ! the primroses with faces that looked from
    lonely places
  Wistfully on me, pearly with morning's early
    dew !
When I dreamed, as children dream, by that
    legendary stream
  Where, agleam in shining mail, the slender
    dragonflies, I knew,
Served our freaksome Irish fairies for steeds, as
    through the reeds
  They flitted on their blazoned wings, in mail
    of green and blue.

III

Oh ! the cowslips in the grass, where the sun-
    shine seemed to pass
  Like Spring's young life through all things,
    in the golden afternoon !
Their scent, like Spring's first honey, made all the
    fields more sunny,
  And fairy money was their gold, that left me
    poor too soon

Of my wealth gained in the meadows of the Spring,
    when I was king,
  With a cowslip crown upon me in the golden
    afternoon.

IV

Oh ! the daisies, when they came with their
    stars of silver flame,
  The baby buds, in green with crimson caps, by
    fairies drest !
Their breath of childhood lingers in my heart,
    as on my fingers
  Their smell when first I picked them in the
    pastures of the West ;
And when memory moves my longing for flowers
    of childhood's hours,
  The Spring comes rushing in my blood—they
    blossom in my breast.

III
SUMMER
I

Over the Wicklow hills the sun's vast blaze
  Palpitates in the abyss of azure bright ;
Dim through the splendour, in a pearly haze
  The glowing woodlands loom. Slow sail the
    white
Swan-breasted argosies the ocean calm

Of the blue air, their shadows drowsily
  Moving like dreams over the fields and
    flowers ;
And every field is pasture for the bee,
Each flower a blithe voice in the fragrant psalm
  Antheming earth's delight in summer hours.

II

Like spirits clothed in light they shine and sing,
  In heaven's own loom woven are the robes they
    wear,
Angels on every wind grace to them bring,
  And back to heaven their sweet oblations bear.
The basking thyme sheds balm about my feet ;
  The yellow iris o'er the marshy ground
    Flames, where the river wanders through
      the dale ;
  The woodbine her grave incense breathes
    around ;
Red poppies blaze among the sunburnt wheat,
  And silver lamps gleam where the bindweeds
    trail.

III

But oh ! the roses ! Here hot afternoon
  Sleeps with her winds in this lone woodland
    glade
Where shine the roses. Ah ! fade not so soon,
  Sweet flowers, each winsome as an Irish maid.

For when your last buds wane, and withered
be
  Your   frail   immaculate   petals   red   and
    white,
    This nook your delicate fragrance makes
      divine,
  Will seem the temple of a lost delight ;
Where, while ye breathe, to breathe is ecstasy,
    Embalming your brief hours in memory's
      shrine.

IV

The sun's heart still throbs through the luminous
    haze,
  I wander through the lost land of a dream ;
Heaven stoops to embrace earth, as she stands at
    gaze,
  Wondering at her own beauty in the stream.
Summer in triumph comes to celebrate
  In magic robes her druid mysteries here ;
    I feel the drowsy glamour of her eyes—
  Time swoons, earth dreams. What ancient
      gods appear ?
What mystic rites ?   What Kings in solemn
    state ?
    What Bards, what Heroes from their grave-
      mounds rise ?

V

O Land of Dreams !   O haunted Innisfail !
  O Land enchanted for a thousand years !
O forlorn Land where sings no nightingale,
  Counting thy woes on rosaries of tears !
Before me, cloudlike, sail wild visions by :
  High tragedies of passionate love and hate :
    Battles and festivals ; heroic deeds,
  Orgies of crime.   Some unappeased fate
Hangs like dumb thunder in the brooding
    sky,
    And phantom fears come stalking through
    the meads.

VI

I wake—how far away !   How long ago
  I roamed, that summer day, my spirit aflame
With youth, ambition, hope, the rapturous glow
  Of courage born, when to my heart Love
    came,
Singing the song that makes this world of ours
  Beautiful as a new-created star !
    Yet still, though Time, the spectre with grey
    hair,
  Bears me each day from youth's glad fields more
    far,
I hear that song Love sang among the flowers,
  And pay no homage to the fiend Despair.

IV

AUTUMN

I

Now is the season of rewarded toil,
  When sunburnt labourers reap to sow again,
And each lean handful cast into the soil
    Waits its rich usury; where the loaded wain,
      Heavy with harvest, lately left its track ;
  For Mother Earth smiles on each golden grain,
      Pledge of man's trust in her who gives him
        back
An hundredfold for one spared from her spoil.

II

What do men reap now in our Land of Dreams ?
  What do they sow ?   Here, over stubbles, leas,
And hills, a sultry mist of sunshine seems
    Deeply to brood, wakening old memories :
      Sad, patient eyes, in faces pinched and pale,
  Haunt me from days when Ireland's enemies,
      Famine and fever, in the Golden Vale
Ravaged and slew, where Suir still flows and gleams.

III

Those days grow dim, and Ireland wakes at last
  Out of her Great Enchantment, and her eyes
Turn from vain brooding o'er the bitter past,
  While in her dauntless heart new hopes arise ;

New songs, like streams outleaping from
    springs,
Fill her glad vales with music, as though her
    skies
    With mellower music hearten him who sings ;
The Nation's blood begins to flow more fast.

IV

Now is our seedtime, when the sering leaves
    Whisper low dirges for the days gone by,
With their dead children, to each wind that
    heaves
    The baring boughs. All things outworn must
    die,
    Yet, dying, quicken, as their life they yield,
Earth and the air with a new potency ;
    And every seeds finds in the furrowed field,
Bare earth to-day, food for to-morrow's sheaves.

V

WINTER

I

Oh ! those nights, those Winter nights
    By the fire, when the sweet brown turf-sods
    glowed ;
When the punch went round, and uncanny sights
    I saw in the flickering shadows, while flowed
The talk when a neighbour or two dropped in ;

Or maybe old Tom the Fiddler would come,
With : " God save all here ! " and glad welcome
    win
    To a seat by the hearth, in our farm at home.

II

" Tom the Rover," " Tom of the Tongue,"
    That could reel off stories, cap jest with jest,
Tom the crony of old and young,
    Tom who could hold his own with the best.
Oh ! the keene, or the lilt of the strings when he
    played,
    When the girls came wheedling for " one more
    tune ! "
But God help the fools of whom hares he made !
    Try a fall with Tom, and he grassed you soon.

III

Oh ! the stories I heard from him :
    Tales of Kings in the days of old,
Merrows, changelings, and spectres grim,
    Tales that made my young blood run cold,
Tales of humour, tales of romance,
    Of faithful lovers at odds with fate,
Tales of the Irish Brigade in France,
    Tales of the horrors of Ninety-eight.

IV

Strange were the sights old Tom had seen :
"The Headless Coach," and the Leprechaun,
And the fairies' court, where he danced with their
Queen,
When into her magic hill he'd gone.
And "beyant by the bridge," one moonlit night,
There crouched the Banshee by the water side,
"With a freckled face, an' she all in white,
Thryin' over her keene for O'Neill that died."

V

Oh ! the rambles I had with him !
He taught me the ways of beasts and birds ;
For he loved them all, fly, or walk, or swim,
Made me know the lives we but docket with
words.
If Tom had his dreams he had eyes as well
For the world God fashions for man's high
school,
The world that spins between heaven and hell,
And His scholar, Tom, was no book-learn'd
fool.

VI

O Tom, 'twas yourself made me laugh and cry !
When our tunes come singing now in my ear,
The old days come back, and clear to my eye
The old place stands there, and the dead appear.

They welcome me home at the door.   I grasp
   My Father's hand, and his hearty voice
Breaks on my name ; I feel the clasp
   Of my Mother's arms by that door of joys !

VII

Ah ! that door of joys ! it opens for me
   Only in dreams, and never more
Will open on earth, save when memory
   Brings back the days I have lived before.
Ah ! the life we lead here from day to day
   Is but a struggle for life, it seems,
That finds us callow, that leaves us grey,
   Our spirits dwell in the Land of Dreams.

VI

A FENIAN'S RETURN

(Inscribed to the Memory of John O'Leary)

I

From exile in a Land of the Stranger,
   I come, as from long voyage, eagerly,
To her port with many a scar of many a billow,
   A ship comes flying, singing o'er the sea;
Safe bearing in her weathered hull, storm-
      battered,
      Her cargo of things rare,
As in my heart, their golden shrine, unshattered,
      My shipwrecked hopes I bear.

II

And here I stand, a stranger, yet no stranger,
 In Ireland, on the soil where first I knew,
In the vision and the glamour of life's morning,
 The silent consecration of her dew ;
The dreams that came, like angels, in her sunlight,
  Ghosts in her twilight grey ;
The mystery and sadness of her moonlight,
  That was dearer than the day.

III

The sun fills heaven and earth with his last glory,
 And, like phantoms, through the veil of golden
  mist,
Loom the Connemara mountains, huge and
  solemn,
 Hewn out of heaven's aerial amethyst.
Plain and mountain dream, entranced in subtle
  splendour,
  Bog and pasture still the same,
Gleam through miles of glowing light, and
  shadows tender
  In the palpitating flame.

IV

And the sunset-wind comes wandering out of
  Dreamland,
 That Dreamland where I wandered long ago,

With whispering in my ear and ghostly singing,
   Druid words, and dirgelike music, sweet and
     low,
Comes from far away, where lilies white are
     sailing
   On waters vast and cool,
Comes o'er cotton-grass and myrtle softly wailing,
   And through rushes by the pool.

V

In the bog stand three lonely pine-trees,
   Waifs of fortune, planted there by Fate's grim
     choice,
And the wind wails o'er the bog, and in their
     branches,
   And thrills me with solitary voice ;
Like the Spirit of an ancient Desolation
   It comes wailing o'er the West,
And the burden of its ancient lamentation
   Is echoed in my breast.

VI

The wind wails o'er the bog, and in the pine-trees,
   With an Irish note of sorrow, soft and wild,
And old memories of dead days come with its
     wailing,
   Till the heart in me is weeping like a child.
It wafts to me the smell of turf-sods burning

In some cabin far away,
And the homelike Irish odour sets me yearning
For a hearth—cold many a day.

VII

Oh ! the story of my home, the dismal story,
　　The story of a thousand homes like mine :
The four walls in their grave-grass, cold the hearth
　　　　stone,
　Dead my kin, or driven like felons o'er the
　　brine !
Raise the keene, O wind ! for Ireland's ancient
　　sorrow,
　　O'er the desolated West !
Raise the keene for our dead hopes of her to-
　　morrow,
　　The pale treasures of my breast !

VIII

Yet, like sweet, remembered kisses of my Mother,
　I feel each Irish sight, and scent, and sound ;
Like her love I feel the tender Irish twilight
　With gentle consolation clasp me round.
Oh ! the magical, drear beauty of this lone land,
　　Oh ! its welcome, sad and wild !
To the Mother's breast of Ireland, of my own land,
　　I come, weeping like a child !

D

VII

TIR-N'AN OG

I

On a cliff in the West, the shy wild West,
The ecstatic, tender, desolate West,
Sits, in a nook where the sea-pink shakes to the
    surges
Thundering far down, a Boy.

II

Far before him,
Thronging the dusk-blue waste of waters,
Foam on their way, like untamed sea-horses,
Rearing, plunging, the giant waves.
Over the waves uncouthly careering
Loom in the gleaming amber sky
Grey clouds : in their smouldering fringes
Fiery embers of sunset, fading,
Turn ashen pale.

III

All alone sits the Boy, and gazes,
Dumb, with the wistful eyes of a peasant—
Sits, while the memoried blood of Kings,
Long lines of legendary Kings,
Whispers to his heart that listens
Wordless magic lore, as he gazes,
Dumbly dreaming.

IV

Far below him,
Landward, with heaving, gleaming shoulders,
Charge, with a thousand miles of onset,
In crested legions, the ocean-rovers,
The huge Atlantic waves.

V

Bellowing, foaming, the ocean-rovers,
The moon-adoring, fanatic waves,
Armed with the sea's eternal thunder,
Swoln with the sea's mad conqueror's lust,
Storm at the bastions of the land,
Ever shattered, advancing ever.

VI

Fresh blows the wind, the wind of the West,
The Irish wind ! Like a lusty lover
He woos on the crags the tufted sea-pink,
With sea-salt kisses ;
And high on the cliff's brow he overmasters
With fierce caresses the lissome cliff-grass,
That quivers and bends, as she vainly wrestles,
Faintly hissing.

VII

O wizard wind, alchemic wind,
Seed-bearing wind of change ! O wind whose
    seeds are dreams !

O brine-soaked, soft, caressing wind !
The Boy too feels it over him swooping,
With downy wing-strokes and gentle
    buffets,
And moan in his ears, as of far sea-music,
A vast, invisible owl of the sea ;
And his Irish blood exults in the wind,
And sings in his veins as the wind blows through
    him.
It comes, through sad farewells of day,
From the Land of the Sunken Sun,
Tir-n'an Og, fathoms down, whelmed by the
    insolent sea,
A thousand fathoms down.

VIII

But, when the Magian Sun, to walk the Western
    waters,
Dons his enchanter's robe, and pacing the cold
    waves,
From Ireland turns his face, Tir-n'an Og, fathoms
    down,
Feels his faint smile of dawn, and rises dim, and
    sits
A spectre on the waters—the Land no voyage
    makes,
The Land of Youth !

IX

The West-wind blows, blows
Over Ireland, The Land of Dreams,
Bearing dreams from the Land of Youth ;
And the Boy sits there, and dreams
Till the spirit of youth within him
Goes forth on airy wings, a measureless
    way,
As he dreams—dreams.

X

Twilight comes, and the stars
Shyly peep through the purpling heavens
And the lone Evening Star,
Thridding the waning, withering clouds,
In gentle splendour, slowly,
Follows, dreaming, the steps of the Sun ;
And she casts her silver spell
On the roaring waves, and their giant voices
Boom with a drowsier thunder.
Then, leaving the sea, the ghostly sea-gulls
Gleam, and fade, and suddenly vanish ;
And high in air, unseen, the curlews
Pass with a desolate cry ; and shyly
Sad-eyed seals, brown dogs of the ocean,
Sleek from the sea on the rocks come
    landing.

XI

And the Boy feels deep within him
Longings vague, like eerie harp-notes,
Wake at the curlew's whistle bleak,
And the soft bark of the seal ; and with longing
Swells his heart, as he sits and gazes,
Alone with his dreams, and the murmuring sea,
And the beautiful, sad stars.

SONGS

MEETING

I

O come to me in the morning, white Swan of the
    thousand charms,
  Or come to me in the passion of day, the rapture
    of noon,
Or come to me in the twilight hour, sweet Longing
    of my arms,
  In the hush when day kisses night, our two
    hearts beating one tune !

II

Though Time on his owl-soft wings bring parting
    of our feet,
  Oh ! never my heart from yours will wander,
    come day, come night.
And never my lips forget your kiss that the world
    made sweet,
  Or my heart the song of my love in that hour of
    its young delight !

PARTING

I

You come, and the little rhymes come singing in
my heart,
And where you are their music wakes trembling
in my breast ;
When you go from me, O my sorrow ! they
spread their wings and depart,
Like birds from a lonely nest.

II

They fly to where you make summer, and leave
me cold,
Their nest forsaking, they leave me cold and
alone,
And my heart is a lonely sorrow, a sorrow not to
be told,
Its music a weary moan !

A SONG OF THE RAIN

(A Girl stands at a window)

I

The rain, the rain, the rain upon the pane,
How it spirts and ceases,
As the spite of the gale increases,
Then pauses and dies again !

II

The rain-drops fallen out of the skies
  Hang upon the pane,
Gather, and fall slowly, like tears from lovers' eyes
  When they know their weeping is vain.

III

The rain, the rain, the rain from over the plain
  Comes drenching, splashing
The pane, as the lightning flashing
  Leaps out, and is gone again.

IV.

The rain-drops pine for their home in the skies,
  And vanish from the pane ;
Yet still my tears are falling slow from these
    lonely eyes,
  Though I know my weeping is vain.

VOICES

I

Oh ! the voices of the wind, the soft sweet voices,
  The melancholy voices of the wind,
Bear me gently to the peaks of ancient vision,
  The lone and silent mountains of the mind ;
And the spirit of old Ireland to my spirit
  Speaks like solitude, and desolately fills
Their silence with the passion I inherit
  From her valleys and her hills.

II

Pale Kings, and hoary Druids in procession
  Pass me sighing, with old sorrow in their eyes ;
While the wind, the passionate wind, with fitful
    wailing
  In his airy tongue of mystery replies.
Grave Kings, and Bards, and Druids without
    number
  Pass by me with the wind whereon they pass,
Sweeping o'er me like a terror felt in slumber,
  As a windflaw sweeps the grass.

III

The Danann gods pass by, majestic phantoms,
  Like shining clouds, bright children of the
    morn ;
But the gods of gloom have dimmed their ancient
    splendour,
  Where, like wizards, in their tombs they dwell
    forlorn ;
Where their ·beauty they have hidden from
    derision,
  Whence they wander, veiled in storm or twilight
    grey ;
But their beauty still shines on the peaks of
    vision,
  And shall never pass away.

IV

There the Daghda walks the wind, the great
    Mor Riga
    Floats beside him to the hosting of their
    clan,
Angus Ōg is there, grey Lir, Bōv Derg, and
    Cleena,
    Queen of the moaning wave, and Manannan ;
Their voice is on the winds, their druid power
    Enchants with youth and love the Land of
    Dreams,
Their beauty and their glamour are the dower
    Of her mountains, vales and streams.

V

There is music on the winds and o'er the waters,
    They are singing still, the wandering Swans
    of Lir,
Silver-pure the voice of love-inspired Fianola,
    Through the long night of enchantment ringing
    clear ;
Like the voice of Ireland's heart she makes the
    nightwind
    Ache with wild hopes that in her breast are
    sore,
Till the red wind from the East, her spirit's blight
    wind,
    Shall have power to blight to more.

VI

There are voices on the peaks of ancient vision,
   They call the dreamers in the Land of Dreams ;
The young men hear, and wake, and in the
      morning
     Go singing through her vales and by her
      streams ;
Making music that shall win the world hereafter,
   Making songs that shall go ringing down the
     years
Of tears that weep within the house of laughter,
   Of joys baptized in tears.

THE LIANAN SHEE

(A Tragedy of Dreams)

I

She waits for me upon Death's gloomy shore,
   Pale, in that pale and lonely grove where
     dwell
Those who have set for portress at Love's door
   Jealousy, stern and unappeasable.

II

She sends me bitter and remorseful dreams,
   That ice the wholesome rivers of my blood,
Crawling about my brain on their cold streams,
   With endless memories in the sluggard flood.

III

I walk in dreams by a dark raging sea,
  And she beside me with implacable face,
Dead, with wide lids where through gaze wistfully
  The accusing eyes, and through my heart they
    gaze.

IV

I lie in dreams as in a living tomb,
  And she, death-pale, her cheek with tears long
    marred,
Comes hovering like a vampire through the
    gloom,
  Craving some comfort, but my heart is hard.

V

She hunts my soul in dreams ; the hounds of
    thought
  Chase me through dense thickets of tangling
    thorn,
The woods of old remorse—till I am caught,
  And wake, still shuddering, in the ghastly
    morn.

THE NAMELESS ONES

I

Through the stately Mansions of Endeavour
Blow the winds, the sleepless winds of wild desire;

And the mansions in their fashion change for
ever,
Replying to the sighing of the winds of wild
desire.

II

All around the Mansions of Endeavour
Flow the waters, deep and strong, of wild desire ;
And fair dreams out of their waves are born
for ever,
The daughters of the waters, deep and strong,
of wild desire.

III

Deep below the Mansions of Endeavour
Glow the flames, the passionate flames of wild
desire ;
And the building-stones, like opals, change
for ever,
Their hues, while slow they fuse within the flames
of wild desire.

IV

For the Nameless Ones come building and
destroying,
In the winds, and rushing waters, and fierce
flames of wild desire ;
And their passion moulds that music, ever
changing, never cloying,
Which is life in all the worlds, in man's heart
a wild desire.

THE HOUR OF FATE

I

Things dead and things unborn are flying,
   And thinly wail on the wind tonight,
Like hungry changelings I hear them crying
   Round the Dark Moon's den in the wan star-
      light.

II

My Saint and Angel have hid their faces,
   My dead sins daunt me with spells tonight,
And sins unborn tempt from unseen places,
   Their glamour works in the wan starlight.

III

The past betrays me, the Future thralls me,
   Fate's hour of power is my hour of blight ;
My frail soul falters—the dread voice calls me,
   The deed I hate I shall do tonight.

THE SUMMONS

O hosts without a name! O unappeasable powers !
O wandering forms of Love, and Beauty, and
      Heart's-ease !
Why is it ye disturb with dreams men's fading
      hours ?
Why is it still the promise, never the gift, of
      peace ?

Your music, your wild singing, came to me out
    of the air,
Alluring, promising, in one mysterious word
Of the great Voice that thrilled old Silence in her
    lair,
Ere the stars for their first flight their mighty
    wings had stirred :

One summons from that realm where things
    unuttered sleep
With the unawakened Beauty hidden from
    desire,
Challenging, maddening me, mocking all things
    that weep,
Till my spirit was a wild wind, my heart a wind-
    blown fire.

My heart was an eddying flame, my spirit a rush-
    ing wind,
Fierce joy, fierce pain, seized me in that mys-
    terious word ;
My heart consumed my life, my spirit left me
    lonely,
Following your sweet alluring song—left me
    behind,
Knowing not where I was, or went ; believing
    only
The vision that I saw, the music that I heard.

The sunset's dying glow was paling in the
    sky,
And twilight, from the visionary land where
    silence dwells,
Stole o'er the gleaming fields, shedding tran-
    quillity
Like dew, o'er bawn and pasture, o'er woods and
    ferny dells ;
But lingering day's farewell grew sad with all
    farewells.

Following the sun's footsteps through the heavens,
    where yet no star
Heralded Night, that now with all her hosts drew
    nigh,
Only the Planet of Love shone in the delicate
    sky,
Only the Planet of Love looked sad from heaven
    on me ;
While through the deepening gloom, over the
    hills afar,
Throbbed a faint orange flame. The ancient
    mystery
Of day's decline entranced the earth. Light's
    quivering wand
Drew from the fields of air their tenderest new-
    born hues,
And made the earth divine.

There in the hallowing gleam,
Beside her cottage door I saw my Mother stand,
At peace with age.   Numb woe for all things I
    must lose,
Following the airy music, following the flying
    dream,
Troubled my heart.   The cows trooped to the
    milking shed,
Lowing ; the grave poplars, and the sallies by the
    stream,
Felt the sad spell of the sky ; but I was as one
    dead,
And all familiar things I loved phantoms did
    seem.

The old place knew me no more—the solitary
    ghost
Haunting the fields awhile.   A robin from a tree
Warbled his last sweet rapturous litany.   The
    host
Of airy singers calling troubled not him, I knew ;
But only me.   And there, in the sweet twilight
    hour,
My Love was waiting me ; whom those wild
    voices drew
Away from home and her ! And now their
    magic power
Made me but as a billow when the moon compels ;

My heart grew drowsy—closed, when closed each
    innocent flower,
My chilling heart shut close. They called—
    called through Love's hour—
They called, and I must follow, lured by their
    wildering spells ;
And the farewell of day shone sad with all fare-
    wells.

THE QUEST

I

The thin rain is falling,
    With a sigh the reeds quiver,
And the cow-herds are calling
    Beyond the dark river.

II

There is gloom in the sky,
    In my heart desolation,
As the cold mist creeps by
    With a dumb lamentation.

III

Like a bird to her nest
    I came, weary of roaming,
With a fear unconfest
    I sped on through the gloaming.

IV

From the ends of the earth
  Oh ! the longing that drew me
To the place of my birth,
  To the fields that once knew me ;

V

To my home ! the bare walls
  Of my dream have bereft me,
The chill spectre appals
  The lone days that are left me.

VI

There is gloom in my heart,
  . In my home desolation,
Like a ghost I depart
  With a dumb lamentation.

FAIRY GOLD
(A ballad of Forty-eight)
I

Buttercups and daisies in the meadow,
  And the children pick them as they pass,
Weaving in the sunshine and the shadow
  Garlands for each little lad and lass ;
Weave with dreams their buttercups and daisies
  As the children did in days of old ;
Will the dreams, like sunlight in their faces,
  Wither with their flowers, like Fairy Gold ?

II

Once, when lonely in life's crowded highway,
  Came a maiden sweet, and took my hand,
Led me down Love's green delightful byeway,
  Led me wondering back to Fairyland.
Ah ! Death's envious eyes that light on lovers
  Looked upon her, and her breast grew cold ;
Now my heart's delight the green sod covers,
  Vanished from my arms like Fairy Gold.

III

Then to Ireland, my long-striving nation,
  That poor hope life left me still I gave,
With her dreams I dreamed, her desolation
  Found me, called me, desolate by that grave.
Once again she raised her head, contending
  For her children's birthright, as of old,
Once again the old fight had the old ending,
  All her hopes and dreams were Fairy Gold.

IV

Now my work is done, and I am dying,
  Lone, an exile on a foreign shore,
But in dreams roam with my Love that's lying,
  Lonely in the Old Land I'll see no more.
Buttercups and daisies in her meadows
  When I'm gone will bloom ; new hopes for old
Comfort her with sunshine after shadows,
  Fade no more away like Fairy Gold !

A MAY MADRIGAL

I

May comes clad in gleaming gold,
The world grows young that was so old,
All so sweet, all so fair,
Birds are singing everywhere ;
  Come away !
Come sing and answer them again,
Answer, boys and girls again,
  And welcome in the May !

II

Mary guard the woods from teen,
Donning now their virgin green !
All be fair, all be sweet,
Where in the woodlands lovers meet !
  All who love true
Come and charm the woods with song,
Glad voices charm the woods with song,
  And welcome Love in too !

MAUREEN

I

Oh ! you plant the pain in my heart with your
  wistful eyes
Girl of my choice, Maureen !
Will you drive me mad for the kisses your shy
  sweet mouth denies,
   Maureen !

II

Like a walking ghost I am when I come to woo,
   White Rose of the West, Maureen ;
For it's pale you are, and the fear that's on you
     is over me too,
        Maureen !

III

Sure it's one complaint that's on us asthore, this
   day,
   Bride of my dreams, Maureen !
The smart of the bee that stung us its honey must
     cure they say,
        Maureen !

IV

I'll coax the light to your eyes, and the rose to
     your face,
   Mavourneen, my own Maureen,
When I feel the warmth of your breast, and your
     nest is my arms' embrace,
        Maureen !

V

Oh ! who was the King of the World that day
     only me,
   My one true love, Maureen ?
And you the Queen with me there, and your
     throne in my heart, machree,
        Maureen !

A DAY OF THE DAYS

I

Faint red the rowan-berries in the glen begin to
turn,

The wind is whispering to the woods the rune
of their decay,

Those woods where once upon my lips I felt your
kisses burn,

Where we met, and where we parted—it seems
but yesterday.

II

Through all their breathing branches the spirits
of the trees

Whispered of love that day ; and we, breathing
their passionate breath,

Trembled before the flaming veil that hid love's
mysteries—

Where now, alone, I bow before the mystery
of death.

III

Martyrs of Love and Hope we stood, and in each
other's eyes

Read the sweet secret of our love ; and that
transfiguring day,

Which crowned my spirit with grace to bear the
sorrow that makes wise,

From that spirit's Holy-places will never pass
away.

ATHLONE

I

Och wirrasthrue for Ireland, and ten times
    wirrasthrue

For the gallant deeds, and the black disgrace
    of the tale I'm tellin' you !

'Twill kindle fire inside your heart, then freeze
    it to a stone,

To hear the truth of that bad day, and the way we
    lost Athlone.

II

O where was then bold Colonel Grace, and Sars-
    field, where was he,

When Ginkel came from Ballymore with his big
    artillery ?

'Twas fifty battering guns he brought, and mortars
    half a score,

And our half-dozen six-pounders there to meet
    him, and no more.

III

They took from us the English town, yet fighting,
    breast to breast,

We held the drawbridge, one to ten ; for we were
    sorely prest.

But we cheered and charged, and they gave us
    ground, and when their Colonel fell

A good half furlong from the bridge we drove
    them back pell-mell.

IV

We held them till to the Irish town our rearguard
    could retreat
Across the bridge o'er Shannon's arm, shrunk
    by the Summer's heat.
The fuse we lit, then back we sprang ; behind,
    the drawbridge rose,
And the two arches of the bridge blew up among
    our foes.

V

We laughed at Ginkel's shot and shell ; for St.
    Ruth came up next day,
And it raised the cockles of our hearts to see his
    grand array ;
But black the hour when Sarsfield chafed under
    his high command,
For, in his pride and jealousy, he left him no
    free hand.

VI

Small help we got from that French Chief, when
    there he just sat down
To guard the fords, and pitched his camp a mile
    outside the town.
Our guns dismounted, shot and shell thinned
    our undaunted ranks
And with our firelocks, four hard days, we kept
    the Shannon's banks.

VII

We made a breastwork on the bridge ; but they
    burnt it on us soon
With their damned grenades. It blazed like
    thatch in the hot sun of June—
And beams they laid from arch to arch, nailed
    planks on every beam.
They thought to rush our last defence, and cross
    the Shannon stream.

VIII

But one we had, thank God !—a bold Dragoon,
    Custume by name,
Sergeant in Maxwell's troop ; and now to that
    hectorin' Scot he came ;
" Give me ten more to go with me, and by my
    soul," says he,
" We'll try the job, and, live or die, we'll spoil their
    carpentry ! "

IX

" Hoots ! " Maxwell sneers, " wha volunteers ?"
    Out stepped some two score men.
" Fall in then, boys, reserves an' all ! " says
    Custume an' picked his ten.
They gave their souls to God, each man his
    breastplate buckled on,
In the hope he'd maybe keep his life till a plank
    or two was gone.

X

I'll see till death, as I see him now, Custume, as
     brave and cool,
He schemed for every man his place ; for 'twas
     he was no French fool.
Then on the bridge before our eyes a glorious
     deed was wrought,
In vain with our best blood that day Athlone was
     dearly bought.

XI

Five plankers ripped the planks away, a sawyer
     at each beam ;
We heard the steady teeth at work, saw axe and
     crowbar gleam ;
But from the startled English lines arose a sudden
     yell,
From flank to flank the muskets flashed, and sent
     their hail of hell.

XII

We answered with our small-arms ; but 'twas
     little we could do,
Minute by minute on the bridge they dropped by
     one and two ;
But as each man fell a man as good ran out to
     take his place,
And the work went on—my God ! 'twas hard
     they strove to win that race !

XIII

At last the planks were gone, one beam was
      loosened in its bed ;
But man by man fell round it in that murtherin'
      rain of lead.
Custume came there, blood on his face, a crowbar
      in his hand—
O blessed Saints, keep the life in him to launch
      it from our land !

XIV

The heel gives—God be praised, it's down ! We
      saw him stagger then :
" Work hearty, Boys, an' we'll keep Athlone !"
      he shouted to his men.
But his heart blood gushed with those brave
      words. The Shannon's waters bright
Were his last bed, and in their arms they took
      him from our sight.

XV

They worked the lustier for that shout, and the
      beams fell one by one,
But the place was just one slaughter-yard before
      the last was gone.
They shot the wounded where they crawled, to
      leave their comrades room,
Or struggling in the water grasped at the flaggers
      full in bloom.

XVI

Each man was killed twice over, and of two and
  twenty men
But two poor boys, as pale as ghosts came back
  to us again.
We scarce could rise a cheer for them ; for
  'twas like an awful dream ;
But the last scantling, with our dead, went down
  the Shannon stream.

XVII

But what's the use of dauntless men, to make a
  gallant stand,
When all they've won is thrown away by fools
  in high command ?
My curse be on St. Ruth, cold friend in our last
  extremity :
" 'Tis hanging I'd deserve," he bragged, " if
  they took the town on me."

XVIII

But they crossed the Shannon's dwindled stream,
  that left us in their power,
And the town we held for ten long days, was lost
  in one slack half-hour,
St. Ruth died well on Aughrim field ; but ten
  deaths could ne'er atone
For the shame and the blame of that bad day,
  and the way he lost Athlone.

THE FACE OF DREAMS

I

Where may I hide my loneliness and sorrow ?
　Where sings the bird that sang upon the tree,
When you and I were young, and feared no bleak
　　to-morrow,
　　And trusted Love to lead us through the years
　　that were to be ?

II

The days, the years went by, the days we lived
　　and loved,
　　When you and I were young, and sat beside the
　　river,
Glad as all happy things that round us lived and
　　moved,
　　And he heard the blackbird sing, saw the whis-
　　pering aspens quiver.

III

The days, the years go by, like eddies in a stream,
　That seem the same, yet glide from change to
　　change for ever ;
I feel them pass and change, and still I dream and
　　dream
　　Of one sweet face, that save in dreams comes to
　　me never.

A MOMENT

I

" Was that the wind ?" she said,
And turned her head
To where, on a green bank, the primrose flowers
Seemed with new beauty suddenly endowed,
As though they gazed out of their mortal
    cloud
On things unseen, communing with strange
    powers.

II

Then upon that green place
Fell a new grace,
As when a sun-gleam visits drops of dew,
And every drop shines like a mystic gem,
Set in the front of morning's diadem,
With hues more tender than e'er diamond knew.

III

And something seemed to pass—
As through the grass
The presence of the gentlest wind will go—
Delicately through her bosom and her hair,
Till, with delight, she found herself more fair,
And her heart sang, unutterably low.

THE CHILDREN'S WARD

'Tis the Good Shepherd's fold, his holy ground :
  With genial face, between a smile and tear,
Old Father Christmas, bustling on his round,
  With presents for the children has been here.

The Children's Ward : there, in her little cot,
  Her wasted face wise with long suffering,
A little patient girl, a hectic spot
  Branding each cheek, her soul upon the wing.

Poor tiny child ! A grave motherly light
  Veils now her glittering eyes. In mother's
      pride
Clasped to her bosom, lovingly and tight,
  With one thin arm, her doll sleeps at her side.

All sickness now, all pain, all weariness
  Are lost in love.   The dumb thing at her breast
Comforts her hungry heart : in that caress
  Her suffering finds relief, her longing, rest.

MEMORIES

I

Whence, at what summons, what faint-
    whispered sigh
  From life's fall'n leaves, what vanished voice's
    tone,
Come ye, the gentle train of Memory,

F.

In that sweet hour when thought dreams on
her throne ?
Ye twilight elves who people solitude,
And are the undying children of dead hours,
My phanton self dwells with your glimmering
host,
Charmed from night's envious brood ;
Ye crown my days with amaranthine flowers,
And I live on, in ghostly lands a ghost.

II

I pass into the fairyland of dream,
As one might pass into the world we see
Deep in lone woodland pool or quiet stream,
With tenderer skies and mellower greenery.
I tread the mossy silence of dim ways
Where sunshine, through the leaves of long
ago,
Haunts the still glades, and holds in solemn
trance
Long aisles where bygone days
Whisper their tales, and memory's afterglow
Clothes my grey past in splendour of
romance.

III

Ah ! do ye live in me, or I in you,
Memories, that bring me in your phantom hands
A sound, a sense, an odour, or a hue ;

As though the past, eternal in the sands
  Fallen from Time's glass, and even as they fell,
    Caught by Death's angel in his hallowing urn,
      Were garnered there without decay or stain ?
      The day wherein we dwell,
Fled with life's pageant, never to return,
    Is it a dream that may be dreamed again ?

IV

The sweet remembered fragrance of a rose,
  Long withered, in a garden ruined long,
Breathes round me—lo ! the cloudy gates un-
    close !
  I am there again, and hear the blackbird's song
In life's glad morn : a crushed geranium-leaf
  Sheds balm, and through the old house that
    stands no more
      I move, with beating heart, from room to
        room ;
      And where the eyes of grief
Looked in Death's eyes, meet those I loved of yore,
  Truants from time and change, as from the
    tomb.

V

The self within us burns, a lonely star,
  And knows not its own form, sees not its light,
Save mirrored in the shapes passing afar
  From birth to death o'er the abyss of night,

Finding itself in that reflected beam
  Which kindles in the House of Memory
    Her pale phosphoric flame. And round that
      flame,
      Moths in her lantern's gleam,
Appear the ghostly train of things that die,
  Yet piteously awhile evade Death's claim.

VI

As feathers shaken from the wings of Time
  Seem the pale memories whereby we live ;
Lingering awhile, then melting like the rime.
  The self we know as frail and fugitive.
But in God's House weaves Mother Memory
  After Death's feet the web of life anew,
    Creation's dream lives in her arras bright ;
      Where her swift shuttles fly
God shines eternal in each drop of dew,
  All moments live immortal in His sight.

AGHADOE

I

There's a glade in Aghadoe, Aghadoe, Aghadoe,
There's a green and silent glade in Aghadoe,
Where we met, my Love and I, love's bright
      planet in the sky,
In that sweet and silent glade in Aghadoe.

II

There's a glen in Aghadoe, Aghadoe, Aghadoe,
There's a deep and secret glen in Aghadoe,
Where I hid him from the eyes of the red-coats
    and their spies,
That year the trouble came to Aghadoe.

III

Oh ! my curse on one black heart in Aghadoe,
    Aghadoe,
On Shaun Dhu, my mother's son, in Aghadoe !
When your throat fries in hell's drouth, salt the
    flame be in your mouth,
For the treachery you did in Aghadoe !

IV

For they tracked me to that glen in Aghadoe,
    Aghadoe,
When the price was on his head in Aghadoe,
O'er the mountain, by the wood, as I stole to him
    with food,
Where in hiding lone he lay in Aghadoe.

V

But they never took him living in Aghadoe,
    Aghadoe ;
With the bullets in his heart in Aghadoe,
There he lay—the head my breast feels the
    warmth of where 'twould rest,
Gone, to win the traitor's gold, from Aghadoe !

VI

But I walked to Mallow town from Aghadoe,
    Aghadoe,
Brought his head from the gaol gate to Aghadoe.
There I covered him with fern, and I piled on him
    the cairn,
Like an Irish King he sleeps in Aghadoe.

VII

Oh ! to creep into that cairn in Aghadoe,
    Aghadoe !
There to rest upon his breast in Aghadoe !
Sure your dog for you could die with no truer
    heart than I,
Your own Love, cold on your cairn in Aghadoe.

VERSES FOR MUSIC

WAITING

I

Lone is my waiting here under the tree,
  Under our tree of the woods, where I wait and
    wait ;
Why loiter those white little feet that would bring
    you to me,
  Where are the warm sweet arms that are
    leaving me desolate,
      Oona, asthore mochree ?

II

Oona, the woods are sighing—they sigh and say :
  The wind of summer will pass like a lover's sigh,
And love's glad hour as lightly passes away ;
  Come to me then, ere my longing hope of
    despair shall die,
      Oona, asthore mochree !

A SONG OF THE SPRING

I

The leaves are springing,
The woodlands ringing
  With birds' love-words in Love's golden
    tongue ;

The blue air winging,
Glad larks are singing,
   For Spring is come, and my heart is young.

II

Oh ! the mirth
Of the Spring's new birth,
   The joy that never was told or sung,
As round the girth
Of the wakening earth
   She flies, and laughing makes all things young !

A COMPLAINT

I

Like a stone on my heart grief's come to lie,
Sadly as phantoms my days go by,
   Though shines the sun at our cottage door.
He gilds the corn with the year's first gold,
While through my veins the sick blood creeps cold:
   My Heart's Beloved comes never more !

II

Grief my handmaid, I sit and spin,
With grief my comrade go out and in,
   I lay the table, I sweep the floor ;
But all I do is a senseless dream,
And here a stranger myself I seem ;
   For my Heart's Beloved comes never more !

III

Grief lies awake in my bed with me,
Like dim corpse-candles the stars I see,
  When the moon shines in, as she did before ;
O mother, mother ! her face I dread,
'Tis like the face on my own death-bed,
  Since my Heart's Beloved comes never more.

THE SALLY-TREE
I

There's a sally standing by the river,
  Ah Mary ! why is it standing there ?
  To make a garland for my hair,
For my lover is gone from me for ever ;
  And that's why it stands there !

II

There's a thrush that sits on that sally-tree,
  Ah Mary ! why is he sitting there ?
  He sings the song of my lonely care
For the lover that cares no more for me ;
  And that's why he sits there !

III

The wind comes keening in that sally-tree,
  Ah Mary ! why is it keening there ?
  It keenes the keene of my heart's despair,
For the lover that's gone, that's gone from me ;
  And that's why it's keening there !

AN AUTUMN DAY

I

Shrouded comes Autumn, walking
Through glimmering woodland and waste,
And with misty breath she quells
The leaves and dreams of Spring.
The robin warbles in dripping glades,
On grassy hillocks the swallows crowd,
Brooding their southward flight.

II

For the migratory sun
Deserts his northern nest,
In the creeping chill his last-born brood
Pine for the warmth of his wing ;
And where harvesters reaped and sang
The gaunt o'erteemed Earth
Sees spectres walking among the sheaves :
Season of visions, hail !

DREAMS

How oft in this mad world we lose our way,
Dazed by the glamour of Love's romantic moon,
Or young Ambition's meteors, fading soon,
In the fierce light of disenchanting day !
And yet by dreams we live, our house of clay

Haunted by dead men's dreams.   Dreamers have
    hewn
Columns for Wisdom's temple, where each June
Brings dewy flowers to crown her seers grown grey.
The gods reveal themselves in dreams.   In
    dreams
We feel the unseen Spirit whose power impels
The labouring earth.   To dream is still to hope,
Hope leads our upward feet.   Our dreams are
    spells
To wake the god within.   Dreaming we grope
After the splendour that before us gleams.

BARDIC TALES

THE WAVES' LEGEND ON THE STRAND OF BALA

I

The sea moans on the strand,
  Moans over shingle and shell ;
O moaning sea ! what sorrowful story
  Do thy wild waves tell ?

II

Ever they moan on the strand,
  And my ear, like a sounding shell,
Chants to me the sorrowful story
  The moaning billows tell :

III

For Bala the Sweet-Voiced moan !
  Here on the lonely strand
Fell Bala, Prince of the Race of Rury,
  Slain by no foeman's hand.

IV

Sweet was your tongue, O Bala,
  To win men's love ; your voice
Made sigh for you the maids of Eman ;
  But nobler was your choice.

V

She gave for your heart her heart,
  Warm in her swan-white breast,
Aillin of Laigen, Lugah's daughter,
  The fairest bird of his nest.

VI

Their pledge was here by the shore
  To meet, come joy or pain ;
And swift in his war-car Bala from Eman
  Sped o'er the sundering plain.

VII

He found her not by the shore,
  Gloom was o'er sea and sky,
And a man of the Shee with dreadful face
  On a blast from the south rushed by.

VIII

Said Bala : " Stay that man !
  Ask him what word he brings ? "
" A woe on the Dun of Lugah ! A woe
  On Eman of the Kings !

IX

" Wail for Aillin the Fair !
  Wail for him her feet
Were swift to seek on the lonely strand
  Where they shall never meet !

X

" Swift were her feet on the way,
  Till me she meet on her track,
A hound of swiftness, a shape of fear,
  A tiding to turn her back.

XI

" Swift are the lover's feet,
  But swifter our malice flies !
I told her : Bala is dead ; and dead
  In her sunny house she lies."

XII

He scowled on Bala and rose
  A wrath of the mist, and fled
Like a wind-rent cloud ; and suddenly Bala,
  With a great cry, fell dead.

XIII

So moans the sea on the strand,
  Moans over shingle and shell.
O moaning sea, of many a sorrow
  These wild waves tell !

THE DEATH OF CONLAOCH

THE BARD'S PRELUDE

I

O Strand of the sorrowful waves ! O Strand of
    Bala ! Once more
The wind-swept grass of your dunes is my
    whispering bed, and I hear
The songs your sorrowful waves moan always
    along the shore,
The old stories your winds through the grass
    come whispering in my ear.

II

They whisper, and all the coast is a druid mist in
    my eyes,
And my heart is a glory of flame, like a dew-
    drop's heart, when the sun
Kindles its heavenly colours ; and round me
    clear visions rise,
As the eye within me opens, and my Path of
    the Seers is won.

THE SON OF AIFÉ

Among the pines of Alba was the birth
Of Conlaoch ; when the salt, sad winds of the
    sea,
On a wild night of storm, o'er Scatha's dun
Moaned in the branches ; and around the house
The gulls and curlews cried, ere his first wail
Was answered by the bleak roar of the surf.
    There, by her daughter's couch, with mur-
        mured spells
To stay his coming till the lucky hour
Of birth should look on Aifé and her babe,
Sat red-maned Scatha ; while, without a groan,
The mother lay, hating her child unborn.
With loathing and contemptuous bitterness
She smelt the balmy fume of magic herbs
Cast by the old sorceress on the glowing turf,
And heard the birth-rune wrathfully ; and thus
Storm on the sea, storm in his mother's heart,
He passed the gates of birth.
                            But magic herbs
And chanted spells are weak to stay the loom
Of those grey weavers, in whose gleaming web
Dark powers with fateful dyes the threads imbue ;
And his good hour looked on the boy too late.
    That Scatha knew ; yet cried : '' A child
        is born,

Beautiful in his form, and in his heart
The seed of valour.   Conlaoch be his name—
A Hound of War ! ''
                  So Conlaoch came, the flower
Of a noble tree ; for when in Scatha's School
Cuchullain learnt the mystery of arms :
The seven feats of dexterity and strength,
The nine great feats of valour, of all there
He had the mastery, save of one alone,
Aifé, and her he strove with day by day,
A year's four seasons, and vanquished her at
      last ;
For love had tamed her fierceness, and her proud
      heart
Turned to her conqueror.   Short was the delight
She had with him.   Soon the untarrying morn
She hid from in her lover's arms, yet knew
With every pulse's beat stole ever nearer,
A sorrow on the track of her glad hours
Not to be stayed, came swooping from the East
On silent wings.   It chilled her bodeful heart,
And passing looked on her with its bleak eyes,
And left joy slain.   Cuchullain must go forth
To take his champion's arms from Conchobar.
  Sad was their parting ; and there upon the
      strand
Cuchullain took from Aifé's hand a spear

                              G

Armed with an eastern dragon's venemous teeth
By Bolg, the Son of Buan. " Take it," she said.
" I give thee here no spindle of a girl,
Wherewith she spins man's comfort in soft wool.
Round the red Queen of Carnage, when she
     weaves
The web of death, and spears, her shuttles, fly,
No spear so deadly sings above the slain."
   The ghastliest love-gift ever woman gave
She gave him then. Five were the battle-horns,
Stronger than steel and sharp in point and blade,
Arming its head, and in its raging breast
Lurked the slain dragon's malice.
                    With wistful eyes
She looked upon him, saying, " Remember me
By this, my gift—my last gift ; for I know
That, parting now, we part for evermore.
No more may thou and I in happy days
Meet in these woods, or walk on this white strand.
Farewell ! That spear will be thy last defence,
And keep thy life in many a dreadful hour."
   Cuchullain lightly wielded it, and smiled,
" The voice of all the rivers of my veins
Sings in my heart for this great gift my thanks !
A warrior's life, my love, is not his own ;
But count me fooled by some forgetful spell,
Or some rash vow, if I come back no more ;

Since here I hold death to my enemies
Life to myself.''

              To her he gave a ring,
Saying : '' Out of the mingling of our blood
A proud hope, Aifé, smiles upon us now,
A child of joy, in whom our love shall flower
In such a flame of valour as never yet
Shone where keen blades reap the red sheaves of
     war.

Thou hast taught me how to woo thee as men
     woo
Strong warrior queens ; teach him all sleights
     of arms
We used against each other, when we played
The glorious game of war, the battle-glee
In our fierce hearts. And when the boy is grown,
If I live still, send him to me, this ring
Upon his hand, that we may meet in joy.''
'' That will I do,'' she said, '' though false or
     true
His father prove himself.'' She took the ring
And fiercely clasped her lover, with a kiss
That might have kindled love in a dead heart.
  So parted they, and Aifé from the shore
Waved her sad last farewell, while the swift
     bark
Fled like a gull, vanishing o'er the sea.

THE SENDING OF CONLAOCH.

Before her child was born, from o'er the sea,
In a bad hour, this news to Aifé came :
" Cuchullain weds with Emer."   In her ear,
And in her jealous heart, that message dwelt,
Poisoning the sweet springs of her motherhood
While the child grew.   Love battling with dark
      hate
Strove in the storms of her breast ; yet the boy
      grew,
No blemish on him, beautiful and strong,
The child of love, not hate ; blithe as a fawn,
And fearless as a hound of noble race ;
Yet gently he endured his mother's moods,
And when she raged would coax her from her
      spleen
With some bright roguish answer, deftly shot
Athwart her bitter humour, like a ray
Of sunshine through the lowering of a storm.

    As an oak sapling planted by a stream
He grew and throve under his mother's eyes—
Sad eyes too proud for tears ; now soft awhile,
Surprised by love ; now cold and fierce again,
Sternly she trained him in all games of war,
Till in the School of Scatha every feat
His father did no worse did he, the down
Of manhood on his face.

                            But when his thumb
Could hold his father's ring, grimly she set
That ring upon his hand, and laid upon him
Three champion's vows ; the first : '' Ne'er to
        go back
Before a living man, but sooner die '' ;
The second : '' Never to avoid the proof
Of battle, though the champion of the world
Frowned in his face ; but sooner die '' ; the
        third :
'' For any man's fair word, or threat of death,
Never to tell his name.''
                            Bitter that day
Was Aifé's heart, where, through long waiting
        years,
While never back to her arms over the sea
Cuchullain came, the black witch jealousy
Sat like a carrion bird, with gloomy spell
Blighting the flowers of love, chanting for ever
In hoarse monotonous voice one baleful word,
'' Revenge !'' Now, as the mother kissed her
        son,
And sent him forth saying : '' This ring will
        find
Thy father,'' in her heart she heard that song ;
And, even when on his hand she kissed the ring,
Her eyes hot with the memory of old tears,

Out of the dreary cave of her sick brain,
Where Love lay on his bier, crept a dark thought,
Whispering : " Now let the father slay the son,
The son his father, my false lover's wrong
Shall be avenged at last, and I can die."
So did they part, and Aifé from the strand
Watched Conlaoch's bark over the heaving waves
Flee like a gull, and vanish in the sea.

CONLAOCH'S CHALLENGE

Over the Strand of Bala and the sea
A morning of great sunshine filled the sky,
Making the fathomless deep of tender air
One azure flame, and with soft inward light
Flooding the bosom of each sailing cloud
That slowly on its way voyaged serene,
High o'er the Strand of Bala and the sea.
On the broad Strand of Bala white-capt waves,
Tripping their ancient measure, up the shore
Danced gleefully, and paused, and turning drew
The lazy pebbles down with murmurous noise.
Green leagues of heaving billows, far away
Gleamed in the sunlight, darkened in the gloom
Where fell the shadow of a passing cloud.
The peace of morn reigned in the sunny sky,
Reigned o'er the Strand of Bala and the sea.

There on the lonely strand a Warrior Youth
Came, landing through the surf : the battle-dress
Upon him like the ransom of a King,
For splendour ; like the glory of the looms
In a Queen's house the mantle that he wore.
The cathbarr on his head blazed like a star ;
The beauty of his hair, flame of his youth,
Gleamed on his broad shoulders. Firmly he stood
On his well-planted feet as a tall pine
That grips with its tough root the wind-swept
　　　crag ;
Or moved with springing step like the red buck
Who rules the mountain-glens, and keeps his
　　　realm
Against all foes. Valour and strength and grace
He wore upon him, as the rowan-tree,
Royal by ancient birthright, in the woods
Wears with blithe dignity her coral crown,
And knows not her own beauty. So that day
Came Conlaoch to the strand.
　　　　　　　　　There by the ship
He left his crew, and, striding from the shore
Shone like a Danann god high on the ridge
Of sun-kist sand-hills, terrible as Lugh,
When in his eye kindles the battle-glee ;
Beautiful as young Angus, when he stands
Upon on eastern hill, and wakes the day

With the far-sounding music of his harp.
    O Spear of Lugh ! for what strange combat
      now
Yearns the relentless fury of thy blade ?
O sweet-voiced birds of Angus, bringing dreams,
What dream fires the Boy's heart, as on his arm
He lifts his death-defying shield, and waves
His spears aloft, and far before him sends
The joy of his voice in that clear challenging shout ?
    Beyond the sandy ridges by the Strand
Of Bala, in the lowlands where the cows
O'er the green meadows, by the wandering stream
Of gently-flowing Fane, pastured in peace,
The young men kept the ford for Conchobar ;
Who, far from ruined Eman, burnt in wrath
By Fergus, for the death of Usna's Sons,
Reigned sadly in Dundalgan by the sea.
    Clear to the young men's booth rang that stern
      shout,
And three came forth to meet upon the dunes
Young Conlaoch where he stood. Greeting him
      there,
They said : " O Warrior Youth, come you to us
This day in peace or war, out of the sea ?
From what strange land fare you, on what strange
      quest,
Shining in arms against us, and your voice

Vexing the air with such a battle-cry ?
If it be death you seek, these plains can yield
Stones for your cairn ; if not, you have come
    astray,
Perchance to light on danger."
                      Cheerily
Sounded the northern music of his voice
In his bold answer : " Flower of the valorous
    host
Of Conchobar, from no chance-driven ship,
Ill-steered, or wandering from her course, I come
From oversea, to find my feet astray
In your long-famous Land.   No fear of death
Dismays my heart ; for here I come to seek
The proof of battle, and one to put me down ;
And slain will I before him fall, or take
His glory from him in fair fight this day."
Smiling in scorn they said : " Grandly must sound
Your name upon the tongues of men, fair youth,
If you can match the least whose shield adorns
Our House of Arms.   But shame of ignorance
Reddens our cheeks, asking your name and kin.
What champion comes over the sea to tame
The pride of Connall Cearnach, or mayhap
Win glory from the Hound of Uladh now ? "

    And Conlaoch gravely answered : " Vows are
      on me

Never to tell my name, save to the man
Who conquers me.   Set me before your best,
And I will strive with him until I take
My death from him, or he defeat from me."
   Wondering they heard, and said : " O stranger
      youth,
Great seems your folly, greater still your pride ;
But welcome be the man whose courage soars
A hawkflight over both ! "
                    They left the shore,
And to the booths beside the ford they came ;
There gave him food, and water from the well ;
For mead he would not drink.   They staked the
      field
And built of sods cut from the sunny plain
The judge's throne ;   then bade him name his
      hour
And take his rest awhile.   So passed the time
In courteous talk between them in the shade.

THE FIRST BATTLE BY THE FORD

   The judge was set, the summoning trumpet
      blew,
And Conlaoch took his place.   Then from the
      booth
Came Connall Cearnach armed into the field.

There courteously they met, and Connall said :
" Fair Youth, refuse not now to tell your name
To me—to Connall Cearnach." Brightly shone
Young Conlaoch's eyes, hearing that name. He
    bent
His head in reverence ere he answered him ;
" Great is your grace in meeting one unknown,
O Warrior King, whose fame lives on the tongue
Of mightiest bards ; and for that grace my heart
Sings a proud song of thanks. But save to him
Who conquers me, I may not tell my name.
That is my vow." " O Youth," Connall replied,
" Your valiant words promise as noble deeds."

    Again the trumpet blew ; and then was fought
Between the two a battle that gave joy
To every eye beholding. The swift spears
Flew like trained falcons from their hands ; and
    fast
They raced like hounds over the field of arms ;
Now here, now there, parrying with watchful
    shields,
Leaping aside, or catching in their flight
The darts of death, to hurl them hissing back.
Yet such fine craft they used in their defence
That neither took a wound.
             They breathed awhile
And Connall cried, laughing : " This is the game

Of boys in Scatha's House, and better none
Could play with me than you, O nameless Youth !
But now our eager swords, hungry for work,
Begin to bite their scabbards.   Let us prove
Their valour and their guile in combat now ! "
   They drew their swords, and closed upon the
     green
With feint and thrust, meeting with blade or
     shield
Many a fierce onset, many a deadly blow ;
Until young Conlaoch, baffling with bold sleight
A thrust of Connall's closed, and lifting him
In his tough arms, flung him upon the ground,
Stunned by his fall.
              Then from the Ulstermen
A cry of anger and amazement rose ;
And Connall as he lay groaned with dull voice :
" Youth you have put such shame on me this day
As never man before.   I am grown old.
My happy star pales like a sunset-cloud,
And victory flies to perch on younger crests.
Slay me then !   Death is better than grey years
Among the old men, whose names die on the
     tongue
Of palsied age ! "
           But Conlaoch by his side
Knelt ruthfully, murmuring :   " As soon would I

Slay thee as slay my father ! Grudge me not
My first great hour, or deem thy honour dimmed
By one unlucky chance ; thou, whose proud name
Shines glorious in the everlasting morn
Wherein great deeds live in undying song.
Where is the man who never felt the spite
Of Fortune's treachery ? Who dare talk of
    shame
When on a noble head her malice falls ? ''

    So Conlaoch strove to comfort him ; and he
Smiled a sad smile : '' Mock me not with vain
    words ;
Better the dreams of youth,'' he said, '' than all
Grey memories of brave deeds ! I am grown old,
My fame lies mouldering like an autumn leaf
In winter's fogs. The old fade with their fame.
Enjoy thy youth ! ''

                  Sadly the young men came
And bore him thence in silence to his booth.

THE SECOND BATTLE BY THE FORD

Meanwhile a message to the King was brought
By a fleet runner, with the bitter news
Of Connall's fall ; and ere the day was old
Two chariots from Dundalgan to the ford
Came racing, swifter than two flames of war.

Far off they saw them blaze like angry stars,
As the wind-outspeeding stallions rushed like
    fire
Over the plain, and far behind the wheels
Long dust-clouds rose like smoke. In one the
    King
Rode with the Archdruid Cathvah, and in one
Cuchullain, driven by Laeg, stood like an oak,
Grasping his battle spears.

                    Conchobar now,
Throned on the seat of judgment, set by him
Grey Cathvah, venerable in magic robes.
There Conlaoch, lightly sinking on his knee,
Made his obeisance, and from the grave King
Great was the praise he heard, with flushing cheeks
And youthful joy of triumph in his heart ;
But boldly still refused his name.

                         Once more
The trumpet blew. Cuchullain from the booth
Come shining to the field, and courteously
Greeted the Boy : " O Youth, in feats of war
Thou hast shamed us all this day ! Tell me thy
    name,
And no dishonour on that name can fall.
I am Cuchullain." Conlaoch answered him :
" O Champion of the World, better my death
From such a hand than breaking of my vow !

That were my black dishonour." Cuchullain
    sighed :
" That face is like the face of one I knew—
Where did I see that face ? " A cloud of gloom
Fell on him, as he muttered to himself :
" Dark is my mind, blind is my groping brain !"
Then looked once more on Conlaoch, and sadly
    said :
" Come ! Wilt thou prove on me thy valour now ?"
    Fast flew their spears. The champion care-
    lessly
Played with him as a master, testing him ;
Conlaoch with careful heed of his defence
Watching his play, made answer with a sleight
Fine as his own ; and soon Cuchullain saw
One worthy of his arms was in the field,
And shouted praise. And now, like two red
    stags
Unmatched before, they bounded o'er the grass
Fighting for mastery ; till the sunny sky
Was overcast, and growling from the hills
The thunder swooped, as there furiously still
They fought, and in Cuchullain's breast the rage
Of battle flamed, and dreadful grew his face;
Then to the Boy, with wrathful shout, he cried :
" Tell me thy name, or die ! " From some deep
    voice

In Conlaoch's heart came the revealing word :
" This is thy father ! "   " Know me then by
    this ! "
He shouted back.   A spear flew from his hand
Full at his father's head ; but by his art
Swerved from its mark, and lightly grazed his
    brow,
And singing past him quivered in the earth.

    Then on Cuchullain madness fell.   The lust
Of slaughter darkly blazed in his fierce eyes,
And, grasping in his rage his ghastly spear,
Armed with the dragon's teeth, he cried again :
" Thy hour is come—take from my hand thy
    death ! "
And rashly, in fatal madness, from his hand
He launched the grisliest horror of the world.

    Sudden and grim the end its baleful teeth
Made of that noble game, superb in skill
Beyond all combats fought on Irish grass.

    Not to be balked or stayed, inevitable,
The demon thing flew screaming o'er the plain,
Through shield and warcoat rending its fierce way,
And Conlaoch fell, pierced by five deadly wounds.

    Fast following it Cuchullain cried to him :
" Tell me thy name ! "   He lifted his weak hand,
And showed the ring, read in the setting sun
That gleamed through clouds parted above the
    plain,

As o'er the sea the thunder died away.

  Cuchullain saw, and knew it. His crime revealed

With a swift pang stabbed his remorseful heart.

In sudden vision rose the Alban shore,

And Aifé waving o'er the sundering sea

Her last farewell. Then with a bitter cry :

" My son ! my son ! " he knelt beside his boy,

And kissed his blanching lips, and his great voice

Tender with tears, and broken with wild sobs,

Groaned out : " Oh ! why this horror ? Why the guilt

Of thy dear blood—my own—upon this hand ?

Did she—— ? Black fall my curse upon her head,

Aifé, thy mother, if she planned this guile ! "

  And Conlaoch, pale with agony, panted slow :

" Curse not my mother—though she laid on me

The vow that slays me ! Curse this worm of pain

Your blind desire of victory loosed on me—

Base weapon for a champion ! Curse the false heart

That held my father's eyes from knowing me !

Wonder is in my mind you knew me not,

When my spear turned from you. Not mine the shame

H

This day, falling before you, magic arms
Against me.   Never had you put me down
Without this plague whose fangs burn in me now."
   His tortured eyes looked in his father's face,
And saw such love and anguish of remorse,
It touched his heart.   Faintly he smiled, and
    said :
" The pity and the sorrow of the world
Wail in my breast for you, seeing your grief.
Take my forgiveness, father—and give me now
The mercy of your sword ! "

                         Cuchullain groaned
And pierced his heart with ruthful steel.   The
    light
Fled from his eyes, as his young life gushed forth,
Following the blade withdrawn.   From his marred
    flesh
His father drew the spear, and shuddering
Flung it away ;   then crouched upon the ground,
Pale as the dead, and weak with wild remorse,
Moaned o'er his murdered son :   " Ochone for
    thee,
Son of my youth !   Madness was in my brain,
Base wrath in my heart, slaying thee !   In thy
    fall
I am fallen below the beasts ;   the championship
Flies these red hands of shame !   Curst be the
    spear

That slew thee !   Curst am I who gave thee death,
And knew not him I slew !   I am grown grey
In aging grief !   An outcast o'er the earth
Now must I wander, black upon my brow,
Where honour shone, the brand of infamy !''
  Meanwhile the men who stood by Conchobar,
Watching the end in horror and strange fear,
Had heard that anguished cry : '' My son ! my
      son ! ''
But Conchobar to Cathvah whispered low :
'' Let us be gone—leave him to mourn his boy
While sorrow tames his heart and makes his
      limbs
Weaker than rushes bent before the blast.
But when the hour of tears goes by, his grief
Eased, as he chants with music of sad words
Keening above the dead, madness may fall
Again upon him ; the raging of his mind
Urge him to turn his fury on ourselves,
And many deaths may hap, ere he be slain
By us or his own sword.   Lay thou a spell
Upon him.   Let him quench his agony
Fighting the woundless waves on Bala's Strand.''
  They left him there with his dead son alone,
And sought the booths ; while he with many a moan
Closed the dim eyes, straightened the cramp-
      wrung limbs ;
And from afar they heard him raise the keene.

CUCHULLAIN'S LAMENTATION

I

Ochone, bad are the days
Without my son, without my son !
Ochone for the days before me,
    And the love slain in my heart !

II

My curse on thy Mother, my curse
I lay, because in her fury
The Kings of my race she slew
    When she drank the blood of thy body.

III

My lap sad rest for the head,
My arms round the body's beauty,
My hands red with the blood
    Of him I slew in my madness !

IV

The father that slew his son,
I lay my curse on that father,
May every spear from his hand
    Come back, my torture and wounding !

V

In a bad field I planted
This valiant slip of my body,
In a bitter field it was nourished,
    To bring this curse upon me !

VI

A man's wrath is a flame
That burns and is quenched in sorrow ;
But like venom never cured
  Is the jealousy of a woman !

VII

If thou and I, O my son,
Were playing war-feats together
O Conlaoch, boy of my heart,
  We would ride on the waves of battle !

VIII

But now death-pale are thy cheeks,
Death-cold is thy fair white body,
And the agony of my love
  Devours my heart like death !

IX

My grief will go from me never
Till my bones in the cairn shall crumble ;
It feeds upon my heartstrings
  Like fire in the hoar hill-grasses !

X

Ochone, bad are my days
Without my son, without my son !
Ochone for the days before me
  And the love slain in my heart !

He rose, and his red eyes were shot with blood,
Ghastly his working face ; and dreadful thoughts
Raged in his brain.   And now he might have
    turned
His sword against himself ; save that he found
The fatal spear clotted with Conlaoch's gore,
And fury seized him.   But Cathvah's druid spells
Against him sent a cloud of magic smoke,
And rushing o'er the sandhills to the Strand
Of Bala, there he fought against the waves
All the night long, till far into the sea
He cast the baleful spear, and the sane mind
Came to him once more.   Then slow, back o'er
    the hills
He paced in the cool dawn.

                      Three days they kept
Young Conlaoch's funeral feast, and where he
    fell
They raised his cairn.   Not long Cuchullain lived ;
But on Murthemny heath, wanting that spear,
With spear and sword was basely slain, unarmed,
By Lugaid's hand ;   and Aifé died avenged.

THE CURSE OF THE BARD

Princess Enna :

Truth is not in thee, Brian the Bard,
Thy tongue is bitter, thy heart is hard !
Because my Father will not strip off
From his breast the brooch of sovereignty,
Wilt thou dare to curse, wilt thou dare to scoff
At the golden gifts he has proffered thee ?

Brian :

Let him keep the pledge that he made to me !

Enna :

No pledge he has given thee, thou Tongue of
    Blight !
Hence with thy Pot of Avarice—hence !
Begone from his threshold ; for at his door,
Brian the Bard, thou shalt crouch no more,
Starving for pride, and cursing for spite.
Thy pride and thy wrongs are a vain pretence,
Thy curses fall on thy head this night,
If now thou drink not, for love of me,
The Peace of the Bards, and the end of hate,
In this cup of mead I bear to thee,
Brian the Bard, is my word too late ?

BRIAN :

I drink derision for love of thee !
King's Daughter, for thee I have borne the spite,
While in my heart is a quenchless flame,
As here I starve on ye day and night.
I crave not gifts, I crave not gold,
I crave not the brooch of sovereignty.
I crave that here I may die consoled,
When here I lie dying for love of thee.

ENNA :

Brian the Bard, thy pride is great !

BRIAN :

Kiss then the cup in thy white hand,
And kiss my lips ere it be too late,
And rove with me, as I rove the land,
And I'll pledge in that cup an end of hate.

ENNA :

Brian the Bard, thou art mad with pride!
Shall I, a King's Daughter, fly with thee ?
Shall I wander the world by a greybeard's side ?
A shameful thing thou hast asked of me !

BRIAN :

I tear this beard from off my chin,
Fling this patched cloak from off my back ;

And if thy love I may not win
Laugh in my face, and bid me pack !
Not Brian the Bard in sooth am I,
But Brian, the King of Munster's son,
And as thine own is my dignity.
As children our fathers pledged our hands,
And now thy father his pledge would break,
Would kindle strife between friendly lands ;
But here I lie starving for thy sake,
And here I starve till thy heart be won !

ENNA :

A starveling at my father's door
Might move my pity, not win my heart ;
But never a royal suitor before
Played with such cunning a madman's part.
If thou canst play the prince as well,
Thou might'st scape laughter—I cannot tell.
Stand up, and look me in the face !
In sooth thou seemest in woeful case.

BRIAN :

In woeful case for love of thee,
And the curse of our fathers' enmity.
I dreamed of thee in my father's land ;
Yet what form was on thee I could not tell,
What heart, what mind might in thee dwell,
What fate for me was in that white hand.

But, now I have seen thee, well I know
The Beauty of the World thou art !
I have come through foes for the love of thee,
I would pass through fire to win thy heart,
Rose of the World, wilt thou come with me ?

ENNA :

A hostage wouldst thou have me be ?

BRIAN :

No hostage ; but my chosen bride !
And if thou wilt not come with me,
Here as a hostage will I bide,
Whatever my fate I will bide with thee.
Take me then to thy father's hall,
And let me stand before his face,
Whether he free me or hold me in thrall,
Whether he slay me or grant me grace :
Or kiss the cup in thy white hand,
Let me kiss thy lips ere it be too late,
And pledge we now an end of hate !
Choose now, I bow to thy heart's decree.

ENNA :

Brian the Bold, I will go with thee !

NINETY-EIGHT

Written 1898

I

A hundred years are gone
   Since Ninety-eight.
What has our Nation done
   Since Ninety-eight ?
Shines brighter now the sun ?
   What progress, small or great ?
What victories have we won
   Since Ninety-eight ?

II

Nine hundred years, upon
   The waters, desolate,
Wept Lir's enchanted Swan,
   Driven by the Witch's hate.
Like that enchanted Swan
   Driven by the Witch's hate
Has Ireland drifted on,
   Tossed by the storms of fate.

III

Now brighter shines her sun,
   Her day of sorrow past,
Her long enchantment done,
   She spreads her wings at last.

UNDER THE WHITEBOY ACTS, 1800

An Old Rector's Story

Ay, I was once a soldier, as you've heard,
A cornet in the Irish Yeomanry.
To say what that meant fifty years ago
Would seem, thank God ! to young fellows like
    you,
Like telling tales about some foreign land
In the dark ages. Yes, my memory
Has its black chamber, where, whene'er I look,
There flicker out, shining with ghastly fire,
Some ugly pictures painted on the wall—
Bad sights !
           Now here's a sample : I was once
Riding at night along a country road,
Patrolling with my troop—one August night.
The moon was full, and surely bright and fair
As when she rose on Eden's innocence
The night before the Fall. What brought us
    there,
Out of our beds ?   Well, in the peasants' phrase,
" The Boys was out."   The Whiteboy scare, in
    fact,
Was in full cry, and Ireland in the grip,
Under the Whiteboy Acts, of martial law :
Nothing new, mind ; the district was proclaimed,

And we patrolled it, to repress the crime
Of being out of doors between the hours
Of sunset and sunrise.

               Well, there I sat,
Loose in my saddle, in a kind of dream,
Thinking, I fancy, of the County Ball,
A pretty face—I was a youngster then—
Had made for me a chapter of romance,
To be re-read by that romantic moon.
Oh ! but 'twas wonderful, that moonlight, mixed
With woodbine scents, and gusts of meadowsweet.
An Irish boy's first love, a cornet's pride
In his new soldiership and uniform !
Why, 'twas sheer ecstasy—I feel it still,
As I remember how, athwart my mood,
The martial noise of our accoutrements,
Clanking and jingling to the chargers' tramp,
Chimed in a sort of music.

               The road turned,
And a stream crossed it. On the further side
There was a man, a scared look in his face,
White in that great moonlight. And there he
    stood,
And never ran—the creature never ran,
But quavered out some question : 'tis my guess
He said : " Is that the sogers ? "   Then I saw,
Like a bad dream, the captain of our troop,

(Whom I'll here name " Lord Blank") ride at
    him straight,
And cut him down.   You, maybe, never saw
A man cut down ?   Nor I, till that bad hour.
Well, 'twas an ugly sight—a brutal sight.
The strangest thing was that the man seemed
    dazed,
Made no attempt to run, or dodge the sword,
Shrank rather from the wind of the horse, I
    thought,
His hands held out in a groping sort of way ;
But never raised, I saw, to guard his head,
Till the blow sent him reeling, with a shriek :
" O Lord have mercy ! "   Then he plunged, face
    down,
Clutching and wallowing in a pool of blood.
He spoke no more—just moaned.   'Twas hor-
    rible,
And all the more for something half grotesque ;
You'd never think a man's last agony
Could look so like a joker's antics, played
To raise a laugh.   Yet no one laughed, I think.
We had pushed across the stream.   I saw them
    lift
His head, with long grey hair dabbled with blood.
The sword had caught him under the right ear,
And through the gash his poor, scared, struggling
    heart

Simply pumped out his life.   'Twas over soon.

They laid him down, stone dead, with staring
    eyes ;

And then I saw it all—the man was blind.

Then someone said :   " Lord save us !   Sure
    it's Tom—

It's ould blind Tom, the fiddler !   Sure enough,

He lives just here in the boreen beyant."

Another said :   " He's due to play to-day

In Ballintogher Fair.   He must ha' thought

'Twas mornin', an' come here to clane himself,

Here in the sthrame.   Poor Tom !   'Twas just
    your luck,

Misfort'nate craythur that ye always wor !

Well, you'll chune up no more ;   God rest your
    sowl ! "

We found his stick, indeed, beside the stream.

Then we rode on and left him lying there

Upon a grassy tussock by the road.

An ugly business that.   I never knew

How My Lord felt about that sad mistake :

Such things will happen under martial law,

And ill-judged deeds, done through excess of
    zeal,

The King's Commission covers in such times.

We heard no more of it.   But all that night

I felt myself next door to a murderer,

And rode with a sick chill about my heart.

No more pride in my uniform ; No more
Delight under that ghastly, glaring moon
That showed me Tom's dead face.

                     Perhaps you'll think
This made me sick of soldiering ? Well, not
    quite.
The young mistrust their instinct, sir, when first
Thrust forth new fledged into the great rough
    world.
I was shocked, surely ; but was half ashamed
To be so shocked.

                Then I saw other things
My conscience quite convinced me went beyond
The necessary horrors of this life. For me I felt
From that time forth the uniform I wore
Smother my soul in shame. I changed it soon
For this poor cassock, which, though not so
    smart,
I find more comfortable every way.

THE COFFIN-SHIP

I

Storm, and the moon like a waif,
Homeless, the baffled phantom of hope,
Pale, with a few dim stars
Fighting the scud for a blink, a peep,
Then wanly, a visage of woe,
Searching the sea with her light.

II

At the base of a westward-looking cliff,
Grim bastion of life from the ocean's long rage,
Thunder : a hill of waters, a frenzy of foam,
Black rocks, to the very fish of the deep
Perdition to-night.   Inshore
Back from the foot of the cliff,
Where faint moon-rainbows flicker and fail,
Stands One by a gleaming pool,
Salt from the send of the sea :
With strong heart long abreaking,
And a cry under the stars.

III

Mad, in the storm, her grey hair dank with the
     wind-blown spray
Her homespun gown soaked round her heavy with
     brine,

As her heart with tears—alone,
A woman stands by the pool,
And wrings her hands, and thuds her shuddering
    breast
With bruising blows ; then scans the face of the
    pool,
And tosses her arms aloft, and sends through the
    night
A moaning, heart-breaking cry :

IV

" Norah ahoy ! Kathleen ahoy !
Dhrops o' my heart, come back to me ! look at
    me here alone !
Come back from the say—come back from that
    coffin-ship !
The rats is lavin' her.   Whisht ! do yez hear the
    wind,
Keenin', keenin' ?   Whisht !   Don't yez hear ?
    When it blows
This-a-way, through an' through me, the hunger
    leps in my heart.
The hunger's on me for yez to-night—I want
    yez—I do.
I'm lonely, childhre', I'm lonely—I'm cowld
    without yez this night !

V

Och wirrasthrue ! Your father stuck to the soil.

Why couldn't they make short work—evict us
    into the say ?

The Big House got him at last, the faver, the yalla
    hole,

The pauper's grave an' me down—an' Patsy
    undher the sod—

An' Shemus—I disremember where is he at all !
    ochone !

I'm lonely, darlints, I'm lonely ! Norah, don't
    lave me, asthore !

Come to me Kathleen, aroo ! "

VI

She turns to the pool, and gazes

At the petty wrath of its waters

Vexed by the wind-flaws ; then shrilly

She raves against the blast,

Matching her quavering cry with the ceaseless
    roar of the sea.

She spits in the face of the storm, and threatens
    with arm benumbed

The raging, thundering surge.

VII

She kneels by the pool, and paddles

With weak hand in the water,

Flattering with vague caresses

Its chill evasive face.

VIII

" O wather, wather ! for all you're quiet and
    small,
Sure you're a slip o' the say—the say, with its
    Landlord's heart,
That never heeds for a cry—th' ould slaughterin'
    absentee
Ragin' and roarin' beyant. Aw, whisht ! I
    owe you no rint,
Ould Disolation !   Your rint is that Coffin-Ship :
Take her this night, an' welcome ; but Chris-
    tians isn't your due ! "

IX

She pleads with the pool ; she flatters its heed-
    less ear with wild words ;
She pleads with sobs and sighs for its favour and
    its aid :

X

" But you wather avic, that hould there quiet
    an' fair
Yon dacent small bit o' land, sure you'll spake
    up for me now ?
Make him give back the childhre' !—Sure he's
    no law for this !
Sure he's no call at all to my childhre' ? Norah,
    came back ?
Bring Kathleen home ! "

XI

Then, even as one at last stabbed with a sudden
     word,
Killing a hope long sick, she starts with a wailing
     shriek
Back from the brink of the pool, and crouched
     on the sodden grass
Rocks herself to and fro.

XII

" Mother of Mercy, it's thrue—it's thrue then !
     O God in heaven !
Dhrownded, dhrownded—gone down—gone down
     in the Coffin-Ship !
An' is it your ghosts I seen, my darlints, below by
     the shore,
Walkin' an' smilin', an' cheatin' my poor ould
     eyes wid the light
O' your two sweet innocent faces—the same as
     ever—the same,
An' I here, callin' yez home ! "

XIII

Then, rising at last, she goes from her station,
     with fitful feet,
Moaning, away through the storm.

" Dhrownded, dhrownded, an' gone from me—
    Norah gone,
An' Kathleen gone—the pair o' yez gone this
    night,
An' gone for ever ! Ochone, ochone, for my
    heart !
Ochone for the poor this night !"

THE SHAN VAN VOCHT

I

" There's a Spirit in the air,"
    Says the Shan Van Vocht,
" And her voice is everywhere,"
    Says the Shan Van Vocht ;
  " Though her eyes be full of care,
  Even as Hope's ere flies Despair,
  Her sweet face looks young and fair,"
    Says the Shan Van Vocht.

II

" And she bears a sword of flame,"
    Says the Shan Van Vocht,
" And its flash makes tyrants tame,"
    Says the Shan Van Vocht ;
  " For she comes old rights to claim,
  And old wrongs burn up in shame,
  For 'tis Justice is her name,"
    Says the Shan Van Vocht.

III

" There's a Land I've loved of old,"
    Says the Shan Van Vocht,
" In her sorrows unconsoled,"
    Says the Shan Van Vocht.

" With her thousand hearths made cold ;
But that tale of shame is told,
And she speaks out stern and bold,"
    Says the Shan Van Vocht.

IV

" For a thing shall come to pass,"
    Says the Shan Van Vocht,
" Though her foes have fronts of brass,"
    Says the Shan Van Vocht.
" They turn pale, they quake—alas !
They have seen the Bodach Glas,
And they wither like the grass,"
    Says the Shan Van Vocht.

THE SUNBURST

I

Through the midnight of despair I heard one
    making moan
For her dead, her victors fallen to gain all battles
    but her own ;
I heard the voice of Ireland, wailing for her
    dead
With wailing unavailing, and sighing as she said :
"In vain in many a battle have my heroes fought
    and bled,
Like water, in vain slaughter, my sons' best
    blood been shed ;
For my house is desolate, discrowned my head !

II

In vain my daughters bear their babes, babes with
    the mournful eyes
Of children without father, soothed by strange
    lullabies,
Rocked in their lonely cradles by mothers crooning
    low,

And weeping o'er their sleeping sad songs of
    long ago ;
Whose eyes, when they remember, as the wailing
    nightwinds blow,
Their Nation's desolation in their singing overflow
With the overflowing of an ancient woe.''

III

O Mother, mournful Mother, turn from wailing
    for thy dead,
Grey Sibyl, yet unvanquished, lift up thy dauntless
    head !
O Swan among the nations, enchanted long, so
    long
That the story of thy glory is a half-forgotten
    song,
Lift thine eyes, and bless the living, thy sons who
    round thee throng,
In the hour of their power they shall right thine
    ancient wrong ;
For their love is deathless, and their faith is
    strong.

IV

Thy leaf of many sorrows, wet with thy tears for
    dew,
Emblem of thy long patience, thy champions
    brave and true,

Knights of the threefold Heart of Green, like
    saints the Cross, have worn
Through their nation's tribulation, through in-
    famy and scorn,
We'll blazon with the Sunburst, star of thy
    destined morn,
On our azure's ancient blazure in royal banners
    borne,
To lead for ever the World's Hope Forlorn.

NOTES

Page 1.   The Banshee, "Woman of Faery," appears in
the form of a beautiful woman, keening for the
dying or the dead.   In the poem that bears her
name she is a personification of Ireland—the Old
Ireland of the Past, the Mother of Sorrows.

Page 3.   Stanza 6.—*Moyle* is the Irish name for the
channel that separates Ireland from Scotland.
Stanza 7.—"The Fianna hear." The Fianna
were the soldiers of Finn MacCool, legendary
captain of a sort of national guard in the 3rd
century.

Page 3.   "The Swan Fianola" was the daughter of Lir,
who, with her three brothers, was changed into
a Swan, by the enchantment of their step-mother.
The story will be found in my "Three Irish
Bardic Tales," published by Dent & Son.

Page 6.   Irish Music. The flagger is the Irish name for
the yellow iris, or water flag.

Page 8.   "Lament of Aideen." This poem is her keene
over the body of her husband, Oscur, slain in
the great battle of Gowra. The great dolmen
on Howth marks her traditional burial place.

TIR N'AN OG.

Page 26. The legend of Tir n'an Og, "The Land of the Young," is the Irish version of the legend of the Island Atlantis. The Irish tradition is that there was once an Island in the Atlantic, sometimes visible from the West Coast of Ireland. It was inhabited by a race of happy magicians, beautiful and unscathed by evil, who never grew old. Sometimes their Island floated on the surface of the Atlantic, and sometimes it sank under the waters; but when the Sun of the Earth mingled his beams with those of his sunken brother, the Island rose and floated on the waves. And many who saw it went mad, and sailed in search of it; but were lost or shipwrecked. But some who saw the vision were content with that, and became Poets.

VOICES.

Page 35. The Danann gods and goddesses were the descendants of the Daghda (Father) and his wife Dana, The Mor Riga (great queen), who was the war goddess.

Angus Og, The Love-god, was the Irish Eros.

Lir was a sea-god, like his son Manannan, and Cleena ruled over one of the three magic waves, which roared on the coast of Ireland when danger threatened.

Bov Derg was King of the Dananns.

THE LIANAN SHEE.

Page 36. "The Lianan Shee" is an evil demon, half siren and half vampire, and is a type of jealousy in the poem that bears her name. She is said to have been originally a Nature Goddess.

THE DEATH OF CONLAOCH.

Page 71. This Tale belongs to the last cycle of Bardic
Tales, the Ultonian Cycle of the Red-Branch,
The Men of Ulster, whose King was Conchobar,
" Hound of Help." Con, or Cu, means a hound,
and the great Irish wolfhound was regarded as
the noblest of animals, and therefore the word
forms a part of the names of many of the Red-
Branch Champions. Cuchullain means Hound of
Culan, the great smith, who forged armour and
chariots for the Ulstermen. Cuchullain when a boy
was named Setanta, and once, roving with his
hurl and ball, he came to the workshop of Culan,
where he was attacked by a fierce dog, who
guarded the door. This dog he killed with his
hurl; but on hearing the lamentation of Culan
over his faithful guard, he promised to take the
dog's place and defend the door. Hence his
Champion's name.

The Champion's vow, laid upon Conlaoch by
his mother, is an instance of the strange vows
laid upon the Champions when their training in
all manly exercises and feats of war was finished,
and they " took their spears " from their
teachers, or from the King's hand. These vows
often produced fatal consequences, as they took
precedence of all other obligations. The vow of
Fergus, never to refuse a feast, led to the death
of the sons of Usna, whom he had promised to
accompany to Conchobar's court, and protect
them there.

THE COFFIN-SHIP.

Page 105. This was the name given to the unseaworthy

ships in which such numbers of the peasantry embarked, after the great famine of 1848. The relations and friends who came to see them off, followed them along the Quay as the ships dropped down the Liffey, keening as for the dead.

Page 111. "The Shan Van Vocht" (Poor old Woman) was a personification of Ireland, in the time of her sorrows. The *Bodach Glas* (Grey churl) is here used in the sense of a menacing goblin.

Page 113. The Sunburst was the banner of the Kings of Ireland: a blue ground, with the sun rising from the waves emblazoned upon it; blue, not green, being the old Irish colour. This blue forms the ground of the Union-Jack.